The Red and the Black

*Mimetic Desire and
the Myth of Celebrity*

Twayne's Masterworks Studies
Robert Lecker, General Editor

The Red and the Black

Mimetic Desire and
the Myth of Celebrity

Jefferson Humphries

Twayne Publishers • Boston
A Division of G. K. Hall & Co.

The Red and the Black: Mimetic Desire and the Myth of Celebrity
Jefferson Humphries

Copyright 1991 by G. K. Hall & Co.
All rights reserved.
Published by Twayne Publishers
A division of G. K. Hall & Co.
70 Lincoln Street
Boston, Massachusetts 02111

Copyediting supervised by Barbara Sutton.
Book production by Gabrielle B. McDonald.
Typeset in Sabon by Graphic Sciences Corporation of Cedar Rapids, Iowa.

10 9 8 7 6 5 4 3 2 1 (hc)
10 9 8 7 6 5 4 3 2 1 (pb)

Library of Congress Cataloging-in-Publication Data

Humphries, Jefferson, 1955-
    The red and the black : mimetic desire and the myth of celebrity /
Jefferson Humphries.
        p.   cm. — (Twayne's masterworks studies ; 74)
    Includes bibliographical references (p. 101) and index.ul
    ISBN 0-8057-8352-0 (hc)b. — ISBN 0-8057-8149-8 (pbk)
    1. Stendhal, 1783-1842. Rouge et le noir.   I. Title.
    II. Series: Twayne masterwork studies ; no. 75.
PQ2435.R72H85   1991
843′.7—dc20   91-9597

Contents

Note on the
References and
Acknowledgments

I have used the NAL/Signet paperback edition of *The Red and the Black*, translated by Lloyd C. Parks. All page references in this book are to that edition.

I would like to thank Professor Robert Lecker for asking me to write this volume; John Ballance, for making the photographic copies for the illustrations; and Ross Chambers, who was kind enough to read an early version and whose suggestions improved the book immensely.

Portrait of Stendhal by Ladislas Loevy.

Chronology: Stendhal's Life and Works

1783	On January 23, Henry Beyle (Stendhal) is born in Grenoble to Chérubin-Joseph and Caroline-Adélaïde-Henriette Gagnon Beyle.
1786	Stendhal's sister Pauline is born.
1788	His sister Zénaïde-Caroline (whom he will never like) is born.
1789	The French Revolution begins; the Bastille falls on July 14.
1790	Stendhal's beloved mother dies, and the unhappy years of childhood begin, presided over by his aunt, Séraphie.
1792	The monarchy is abolished, ending the reign of Louis XVI, and a republic is declared.
1792–1794	"La tyrannie Raillane": Stendhal is tutored by the Jesuit Abbé Raillane, whom he would hate for the rest of his life.
1796–1799	Studies at the new Ecole Centrale de Grenoble.
1799	Wins prizes in mathematics and literature and leaves for Paris to seek entrance to the Ecole Polytechnique. Once in Paris, however, he does not take the entrance exam.
1799–1804	Bonaparte, as First Consul, is vested with dictatorial powers. In 1804 he is crowned emperor and enacts the Civil Code into law.
1800	Stendhal's cousin Pierre Daru gets Stendhal a position in the War Ministry. In Italy, becomes aide-de-camp to General Michaud in 1801. In 1802 resigns from the bureaucracy.
1802–1805	Lives in Paris, reads the *idéologues,* particularly Destutt de Tracy's *L'Idéologie*, works on developing his personal

	philosophy. Becomes interested in acting and writing comedies.
1805	Moves to Marseille with the actress Mélanie Guilbert and takes a position with a commercial business.
1806–1808	Rejoins military bureaucracy and is sent to Germany.
1809	Spends time in Vienna and Hungary.
1810	Becomes Auditor to the Council of State and Inspector of Crown Buildings.
1811	Returns to Italy.
1812	Participates in Napoleon's retreat from Moscow.
1814	Assists in organizing resistance to the invasion of France at Grenoble. Napoleon falls and is exiled to Elba; the Bourbon monarchy (Louis XVIII) is restored. Publishes *The Lives of Haydn, Mozart, and Metastasio.*
1814–1821	Lives in Milan on his government pension. Travels to Rome, Naples, Florence, London.
1815	Napoleon returns from exile, is defeated at Waterloo and reexiled.
1817	Meets Destutt de Tracy. Publishes *History of Painting in Italy* and *Rome, Naples, and Florence.* With the latter publication, first uses the pseudonym M. de Stendhal.
1818	The occupation of France ends. Stendhal begins working on his *Life of Napoleon*, which he will never finish.
1818–1821	Passionate and totally unrequited love for Mathilde Dembowski.
1819	Stendhal's father dies, leaving him virtually nothing.
1821	Napoleon dies. Stendhal is suspected of "liberal" activities by the Austrian authorities and forced to leave Milan. Moves to Paris.
1822	Publishes *On Love.*
1823	Publishes *Life of Rossini* and the first part of *Racine and Shakespeare.*
1824	Louis XVIII dies and is succeeded by Charles X.
1824–1826	Stendhal's affair with the countess Curial.
1825	Publishes second part of *Racine and Shakespeare.*

Chronology

1827	Publishes *Armance*. Is expelled from Milan by Austrian authorities.
1829	Begins work on *The Red and the Black*. Publishes *Roman Journal*.
1830	The July Revolution deposes Charles X and replaces him with Louis-Philippe I, of the house of Orléans. Stendhal has an affair with Giulia Rinieri. He asks to marry her and is denied permission. *The Red and the Black* is published and meets a generally hostile criticial reception. Victor Hugo is reported to have said he could not make himself read past page 4. Louis-Philippe names Stendhal consul in Trieste.
1831	Austria refuses to accept Stendhal as consul. He is sent instead to Civita-Vecchia.
1831–1832	Spends most of the time in Rome and Civita-Vecchia.
1834–37	Works on *Lucien Leuwen, The Life of Henri Brulard,* and *Le Rose et le vert* (The pink and the green); finishes none.
1836	Obtains a leave from duties at Civita-Vecchia. Returns to Paris.
1838	Publishes *Memoirs of a Tourist* and writes *The Charterhouse of Parma* in 52 days.
1839	Returns to official duties at Civita-Vecchia. *The Charterhouse of Parma* is published. Works on *Lamiel*, which is never finished. Balzac publishes his very favorable review of *Charterhouse*.
1840	Napoleon is reinterred in the Invalides in Paris.
1841	Suffers a first fit of apoplexy and is forced to take a leave from official duties.
1842	Dies in Paris.

LITERARY AND
HISTORICAL
CONTEXT

1

"History": The Novel's Cultural, Literary, and Political Context

Henri Beyle, whom we know as Stendhal, was born in 1783, in Grenoble, in the southeast of France, near the French-Italian Alps. To be born at this time, anywhere in France, meant that one was witness to the most cataclysmic political upheaval in all of French history: the Revolution of 1789 and Napoleon's subsequent rise to power.

More than almost any other important writer of the nineteenth century, the hopes and aspirations of Henri Beyle as a young man were bound up with the aspirations of the French nation under Napoleon. Young men of the time were aware that the Revolution had opened many doors previously open only to the most privileged; the rise to power of Napoleon himself was a living example of how far merit might carry an ambitious individual. Thus Beyle's sensibility was shaped by the exhilaration of unprecedented opportunity and freedom, and by the glorious spectacle of France as the center of a European empire, but also by the devastating defeat of French aspirations at Waterloo, which led to the restoration of the monarchy. Beyle would begin, but never finish, a biography of Napoleon that would have also been, in grand

3

The house in Grenoble where Stendhal was born.

metaphor, a chronicle of his own projected ambitions and hopes and defeats. This is true despite his stated ambivalence about Napoleon as reported by Prosper Mérimée: "It was hard to know what he thought about Napoleon. Almost always, he was of an opinion contrary to the one being advanced. Sometimes he spoke of him as of a nouveau-riche dazzled by gaudiness, constantly failing to observe the rules of LOGIC. At other times, there was an almost idolatrous admiration."[1]

Apparently Beyle admired Napoleon the revolutionary and republican, but despised Napoleon the autocrat. Probably he felt similarly ambivalent about himself. Perhaps he never finished his biography of Napoleon because he found more direct, more rewarding, more appropriate ways of coming to terms with his personal history: at an ironic distance, through the writing of fiction and criticism. Throughout all those published works, nonetheless, the figure of Napoleon casts a long shadow. Julien Sorel, the hero of *The Red and the Black*, looks constantly to the example of Napoleon for guidance, for consolation, and for inspiration. Three of Beyle's novels—*Armance, The Red and the Black*, and *The Charterhouse of Parma*—chronicle the lives of young men who came of age in the wake of Napoleon; *Lucien Leuwen*, which was never finished, would set a similar protagonist at a slightly later time, against the historical backdrop of the Revolution of 1830 and the fall of the monarchy.

Beyle wrote that "a mad and necessarily unhappy ambition has taken hold of all the French" because of the example of Napoleon's rise from lieutenant to emperor, and of his creation of an entirely new nobility from persons of equally humble origin.[2] For most young men of Beyle's age, who had served, like him, in the Napoleonic military and perhaps risen within it, and for whom Napoleon's success was quite literally their own, the defeat of Napoleon and of France and the return to power of a monarchy that represented centuries of stultifying restriction was a crushing blow and a humiliating disappointment. As a child, Henri Beyle had felt himself at odds with his family and grew to despise his father's petit bourgeois attitudes, according to which conformity was a great virtue and money more important than anything else. For someone of introspective and philosophical bent, like Beyle, the fall of Napoleon would deepen a sense of stoic disdain, of contempt for the vagaries of history and the ways of men.

Even when very young, he identified with the advancing revolution, perhaps because the three people he most hated at the time—his father, his aunt Séraphie, and his teacher, the Jesuit priest Raillane—were horrified by it. He was educated at the Ecole Centrale of Grenoble, a sort of school mandated by the revolutionary government in which paramount importance was given to the new positivism of the eighteenth-century *philosophes*, to reason, logic, and scientific inquiry. Distinguishing himself in literature and mathematics at the Ecole Centrale, Beyle was sent to Paris in 1799 to seek admission to the Ecole Polytechnique. He was received by relatives on his mother's side, the Daru family. Pierre Daru, oldest son of the family, held an important position in Napoleon's War Ministry and secured a position there for Beyle. Abandoning plans to enter the Ecole Polytechnique, Henri Beyle quickly became bored with his secretarial duties and in 1800 joined the army, a move that took him to Italy. He spent much of the year in Milan, where he began his *Journal*. Milan would always be his favorite city, and he would return there after the fall of Napoleon to stay for seven years.

In 1801 he left the army and went back to Paris. He had by this time become preoccupied with literary ambitions and hoped to become a great playwright. By 1806, bored again and frustrated by his poverty and his failure to succeed in commerce, he once more obtained a position in the War Ministry with Pierre Daru's help. He would rise quickly in the imperial bureaucracy, spending time in Germany, Italy, and finally in Russia, where he would be present for Napoleon's great defeat at Moscow. The fall of the empire in 1814 was a serious personal setback for Beyle, ending the most materially, outwardly glorious years of his life. From now on, he would be a writer and something of a literary dilettante, though in 1830, with the fall of the restored monarchy, he would reenter government service as a diplomat. He would return to Milan for the years 1814–21, writing articles for English magazines and art and music criticism, publishing his *Lives of Haydn, Mozart, and Metastasio*, his *History of Painting in Italy*, and *Rome, Florence, and Naples*.

In 1821 he returned to Paris and wrote two important critical and philosophical works: *On Love*, which would have an influence on Marcel Proust's theories of desire nearly a century later, and *Racine and Shakespeare*, in which he deliberately embroiled himself in the fashionable controversy over romanticism by defining and defending his own version of it. Only in 1827, at the age of 44, after a long career as a writer of nonfiction and criticism, and with a fully developed sense of his personal philosophy and literary style, would he publish his first novel, *Armance*. Three years later he would publish *The Red and the Black*. He saw the revolution of July 1830 as a personal vindication, though by this time he was somewhat cynical about politics.

From the time of his first arrival in Paris, Beyle had been reading avidly, working on the development of a personal philosophy that would find expression as what he called *beylisme*. He was influenced by the positivism of the eighteenth-century *philosophes* and the *idéologues* who succeeded them into the nineteenth, from whom he imbibed a belief that rigorous scientific inquiry could lead to real improvement of the human condition.

The Abbé de Condillac and Claude Adrien Helvétius, both *philosophes*, drastically radicalized the thought of the English philosopher John Locke by arguing that all of human thought, emotion, and feeling were reducible to the interaction of physical sensations, and that they could therefore be studied like any other physical phenomenon, according to the laws of science and logic. In effect, they reduced the human being to a network of nerve pathways, but they did so in a spirit of optimism, arguing that this made possible the perfectibility of every man through a correct education. The *idéologues* developed this line of thought further.

Henri Beyle knew one of the *idéologues*, Destutt de Tracy, through his works as well as personally, and considered him a genius. From Tracy, Condillac, and Helvétius, Beyle got the idea that human thoughts and emotions could be understood "scientifically." He coupled this empirical positivism—that aspect of himself which excelled in mathematics as a student—with *espanolisme* (literally, "Spanishness"), that side of him which was lustful, sentimental, exuberantly egotistical and ambitious, which tended to passionate, often unrequited love affairs, and which felt a sympathy with romanticism that was both natural and opportunistic—that part of him, in short, which found literature more rewarding than logic and had won school prizes in literature. Putting the former in the service of the latter formed Beyle's "science of happiness." He believed that it was possible by rigorous observation to discover how happiness might best be achieved and sustained. Much of what he wrote was an attempt to scrutinize every circumstance's impingement upon the happiness of an individual character, whether positive or negative.

The other aspect of *beylisme* was the literary style that he evolved as best suited to this "scientific" study of the possibilities of happiness. Beyle was frustrated by his inability to describe precisely the scenes, the circumstances, the emotions he had observed. He discovered, however, that his first attempt at expression seemed the closest to truth, though it might not be the most polished. Thus, for the sake of "science" and "rigor," he eschewed the obsessive textual perfectionism that was to be demonstrated later by Gustave Flaubert, and did not painstakingly revise and rewrite—though he did, like Honoré de Balzac, often add to his text when correcting printer's galleys. These are the two sides of *beylisme*: the study of the possibilities of happiness, and a method of writing suited to that study.

It of course makes sense that Beyle should have been so compelled by the subject of happiness because his own was so often dashed or impeded by (apparently) uncontrollable circumstances. All of his novels have young male protagonists who share much in common with the young Henri Beyle. He would not write autobiography as such (*The Life of Henri Brulard*) until near the end of his life, but all his books are in one sense attempts to replay the events of Beyle's own life before the age of 30 in the hope of discovering what went wrong, of finding the lost secret of happiness. That the effort had to be repeated endlessly—Beyle was at work on another novel at the time of his death—suggests that it could not succeed, that Beyle's fiction in this respect is a monument to the Freudian compulsion to repeat. To repeat what? the drama of loss, of the defeat of desire, the failure of desire ever to reach and hold on to its true object—but also the drama of the individual seeking to rise above his circumstances in fact as well as in mind, to use his gifts to realize happiness as a fact rather than as an abstraction. That is still the archetypal drama of every individual in the modern age, and happiness still works today as it did when Stendhal was alive and as Stendhal saw it: all human desire comes down to a desire for happiness, according to Stendhal, and happiness is extremely problematic in our age because it depends so much on the desires of others. That theory, quite visible in *The Red and the Black*, as we will see, has held up extremely well, and accounts for much of what is called Stendhal's "modernity," for our continuing to find his novels relevant to our time and our concerns.

His most important critical works, *On Love* and *Racine and Shakespeare*, reflect the same preoccupations that Beyle dramatized in the novels and in *The Life of Henri Brulard*. *On Love* "scientifically" examines the way in which humans fall in and out of love, elaborating a theory of desire with which Beyle made sense of his own experiences and prepared himself to write about desire in the novels. He defined love as having three stages:

admiration, hope, and crystallization. His reduction of human emotion to pure physiology—heavily influenced by the theories of Destutt de Tracy and Condillac—seems a little absurd now, but his analysis of the stages of desire has held up well, influencing Proust and other writers of the twentieth century (of course, it had antecedents as well).

In *Racine and Shakespeare* Beyle came up with a notion of romanticism different from all the others. He defined the romantic as, quite simply, literary innovation. He argued that beauty was relative; the beautiful was anything that seemed to hold out the possibility of happiness, any (potential) object of desire. So beauty was bound not to remain the same from year to year, and romantic art would respond to these transmutations. Classicism, on the other hand, was concerned more with tradition and rules. Shakespeare was the romantic—pragmatic, responding to his audience and his age—while Racine represented the classical impulse, believing in the immutability of beauty and of the rules governing its artistic expression. Victor Hugo's famous manifesto of romanticism, his preface to *Cromwell*, owes more than a little to Stendhal's ideas on the subject. *Racine and Shakespeare* is a theoretical exposition of Beyle's own iconoclasm, his personal hatred of all status quos, of institutions and institutionalized values. The same iconoclasm would characterize Julien Sorel, the protagonist and on occasion Beyle's *porte-parole* in *The Red and the Black*.

Henri Beyle used about 150 pseudonyms, according to the latest count, among them Lisio Visconti, Timoléon du Bois, and William Crocodile.[3] As he himself put it, "Will anyone believe me? I would wear a mask with pleasure, I would change my name delightedly. The *Thousand and One Nights*, which I adore, occupies more than a quarter of my mind. Often I think of Angelica's ring; my sovereign pleasure would be to change myself into a blond German, and thus walk through Paris."[4] The power of names, of language, to reshape human identity, to exorcise the past by giving it a new name, a fresh description, must have been intoxicating to him. It was in 1817, with the publication of *Rome, Florence, and Naples,* that he assumed the nom de plume of Stendhal, the name of a German city, by which he is remembered in literary history.[5]

2

Why Read The Red and the Black?

The Red and the Black is widely thought to be one of the greatest
"psychological" novels. Julien Sorel has always been described by
critics as an extremely subtle and complex character. The novel
has also been praised for its representation of the "mood" of the
French nation following the defeat of Napoleon and the restoration of the monarchy. These judgments hinge on criteria of conventional realism: Stendhal's greatness as a writer would be in
having created characters that are both complex and believable,
that give us insight into the psychology of real people, and in having drawn a historically revealing portrait of post-Napoleonic
France.

I don't, however, find that such judgments—critical plati-
tudes, really—tell us anything interesting or useful about the
novel, or constitute an adequate answer to why we read or should
continue to read *The Red and the Black*. Any novel, any work of
literature continues to be read for as long as there are readers who
find pleasure in reading it. The kind of pleasure we take in reading
a novel is a feeling that it *makes sense* of things for us in a way we
find reassuring or useful; it constructs a narrative order, a story of

The countess Curial, Stendhal's mistress from 1824 to 1826.

the way the world works, that we believe we need or want to know—a story that contains some clue to the secret of "happiness." All of Stendhal's novels suggest, by the example of their characters, that in our culture, we no longer acquire the paradigms of desire from myths, but through the media of popular culture, including novels. Julien Sorel knows what he wants from having read books about what other people wanted—specifically Rousseau's *Confessions* and Napoleon's *Mémorial de Sainte-Hélène*. As the critic René Girard might put it, modern desire functions always by the mediation of a third party, the spectacle of whose desire provides a model and a goad to our own.

Fewer and fewer people read novels at all. Most people who do read choose popular nonfiction (the self-help book) or the pulp novel (romance or horror) over more "difficult" fare. These options—high culture or low—have always existed. The options of low culture are greater in variety than ever before. They include television, film, magazines, and popular music as well as books, all of which contain paradigms of desire that we may take as models for our own. There have never been all that many options at the level of high culture, and there still aren't: some fiction, less nonfiction, a few films, the visual arts, and music, especially, perhaps, opera. Most educated persons with some pretense to acculturation will have their desire shaped early on by the popular media, and only later on refine and polish the beast with more sophisticated, self-aware models.

What do I mean by "sophisticated" literature, as opposed to unsophisticated? Sophisticated literature might be said to show us something about how desire works—and thus about how literature works—at the same time that it solicits our desire (our attention). Unsophisticated literature merely solicits our desire (our attention), thus engaging us in a circuit of desire while allowing us to pretend that there is no circuit, that we are dealing simply with "reality." Unsophisticated literature manipulates our desire without admitting it. Unsophisticated literature, by this definition, may be not only a book; it may be popular music, a television program, a film, or an advertisement.

My argument here may suggest that there is nothing more to reading unsophisticated literature than a kind of pleasurable and willing submission to brainwashing—which is probably true—and that there is nothing more to reading sophisticated literature than a kind of indoctrination or self-instruction—which is not entirely true. There is also, in the engagement with sophisticated literature, a keen pleasure in finding out how desire works, both our own and others'. Why? because we are vain as well as self-interested. Knowledge about the way desire works may be a form of power over desire, our own and others', if only a stoic power of knowing (rather than an active power). If we would make our way more or less safely and agreeably through the world, we had better find out all we can from the best sources. The more subtle and finely tuned our examples and our knowledge, the more empowered we are, if only in a passive sense. That's the best argument for reading good books. But our own desire must be sufficiently acculturated, educated, and prepared by exposure to other sophisticated patterns of desire, that is, to sophisticated narratives. It must be capable of feeling itself implied in the reading for there to be pleasure, for if there is no pleasure, there is little or no understanding.

Stendhal offers us in *The Red and the Black* one of the most subtle, complex, and accurate narratives of desire in modern literature. By accurate I mean that it holds up when tested against experience. Somehow, as critics have pointed out over and over throughout the decades since Stendhal's death, this text has seemed to remain modern for 150 years. We can still see Julien Sorels around us. Readers have continued to take pleasure in his story, to find it compellingly revealing. Claude Roy is not the only critic to have pointed out that

Stendhal is the author, if not of one single novel, at least of one single paradigm, of one single type of novel. Every novel of Stendhal is an enterprise of social criticism and romantic pleasure centered around a

figure who struggles against an unpleasant father (*The Charterhouse
..., The Red ...*) or a charming one (*Lucien Leuwen, Armance*),
shared by two female figures, surrounded by revolutionaries, politi-
cians, and priests (subdivided into two categories: the good-old-wise-
village-priest, and the calculating and intriguing monsignor). Among
the secondary themes, those of presage, of prison, of the plot or conspiracy, are involved with the first.[6]

Perhaps the very simplicity of this formula partly explains its en-
durance: the same, or a very similar, cast of characters has been
the basis for many films and TV shows, not to mention literary
works of high and low quality. Why should *The Red and the
Black* be esteemed any more than these? Probably because of the
keen and subtle sense of irony that pervades it: it contains within
it, and reflects back at us, the very structure of desire that we
enact by reading it. Just as Julien finds out how desire is supposed to work from reading books, so do we, by reading this
one—with the important difference that, in the character of
Julien, we see ourselves doing it.

But this, in itself, is not unique. The classical, "high literary"
novel always deals obsessively with the ways in which desire is mediated and therefore subject to manipulation, from the beginning
of the genre in France with Madame de Lafayette's *Princesse de
Clèves* in the seventeenth century, on through the eighteenth century, in, for example, Choderlos de Laclos's *Les liaisons dange-
reuses*. The latter novel, like others, elaborately explores the
scandal of seduction, of the deliberate, calculated manipulation of
another's desire. What is different about Stendhal's practice is that
he shows how the act of seduction is itself subject to mediation.
That is, the seducer cannot control the ways in which his or her
own desire to seduce is mediated or interpreted by others. The
seducer is subject to the same ironies, the same possibilities for
misunderstanding and being misunderstood, as someone being seduced. This produces comic moments of much greater complexity
than those of an eighteenth-century novel like Henry Fielding's

Joseph Andrews, in which comedy is derived from the situation of an object of desire who does not understand the codes of desire and seduction. Critics have long recognized Stendhal's use of irony as unique, as we will see in the next chapter. It is unique, however, primarily in the sense that he exempts no one from its effects.

3

Stendhal and the Critics

Stendhal's work was not well received critically during most of his life. Charles Sainte-Beuve accused him of lacking "inventiveness" because all his novels had the same sort of protagonist, very similar plots, even similar secondary characters. But Sainte-Beuve, who identified above all with the institutional values and traditions of French literature, could not be expected to admire a writer so vehemently iconoclastic as Stendhal. Perhaps what offended him most about Stendhal was his uniqueness, the fact that he could not be satisfactorily classified with any school of literature, despite having affinities with several. Sainte-Beuve's job, as he saw it, was taxonomic, to identify the species and genus of a writer. This was very hard to do with Stendhal, so Sainte-Beuve finessed the quandary by dismissing him. During its author's lifetime, readers generally found the ironies of *The Red and the Black* too disturbing.

Stendhal did have his admirers, though. Prosper Mérimée, though he found the character of Julien Sorel repugnant, predicted that some twentieth-century critic would discover Stendhal as Garrick had rediscovered Shakespeare. Stendhal himself thought he would start to be appreciated around 1880. It did not

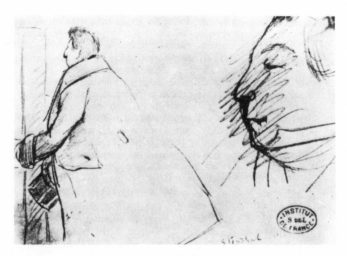

Alfred de Musset did this sketch of Stendhal during his trip to Italy with George Sand in 1833.

take that long, in fact; just before his death, Stendhal would read Balzac's very favorable review of *The Charterhouse of Parma*. Balzac, as well as Mérimée, however, did not care much for *The Red and the Black*. Nobody, in 1830, was ready to see so intimately into the thoughts and aspirations of a character like Julien. By 1839 Stendhal's contemporaries were catching up with him: they had become less squeamish, or perhaps Fabrice Del Dongo, the protagonist of *Charterhouse*, seemed to them more palatable, less raw, not imbued with quite such violent desires as Julien.

The positivist critic Hippolyte Taine would, in the latter half of the century, praise Stendhal's work for its "science" of observation, its relentless empiricism. Friedrich Nietzsche would praise him as "the last great psychologist of France," admiring his characters for their fierce will to power and iconoclasm. In *Ecce Homo*, he wrote: "Stendhal, one of the most beautiful accidents in my life—for whatever marks an epoch in it came my way by accident, never through someone's recommendation—is truly invaluable with his anticipatory psychologist's eye, with his knack for the facts which is reminiscent of the greatest of factual men (*ex ungue*

Napoleonem), and finally not least as an *honest* atheist—a species that is rare in France. . . . Perhaps I am even envious of Stendhal? He took away from me the best atheistical joke I might have made: 'God's only excuse is that he does not exist.' "[7]

Emile Zola would find in Stendhal's theory and practice a justification of his own school of pseudo-scientific, journalistic realism known as naturalism. Proust would rediscover Stendhal's theories about love and his meticulous observation of the vagaries of desire, pursuing them even further—out-Stendhal-ing Stendhal, as it were—in his own work. Writers as different as André Gide and Paul Valéry would find themselves compelled to admire Stendhal's work without being able to say quite why: Valéry wrote that Stendhal had the most unique "tone" or voice in literature, and Gide called Stendhal his "cuttlefish bone": he "sharpened his beak," parrotlike, on Stendhal. Virtually every subsequent school of literary practice has found something to identify with in Stendhal. Julien Sorel has been a hero for everyone from surrealists to existentialists.

The writing style—spontaneous, uncontrived, even conversational—which Flaubert and Hugo, from quite different perspectives, both hated, has proven itself by remaining fresh through the years. Over and over, right up to the present, writers and critics have said that Stendhal's voice seemed to them like that of a contemporary.

So Stendhal has been placed in the canon as one of the great founders of the modern Euro-American realistic novel, along with Balzac and Flaubert. *The Red and the Black* has long been his most widely read novel, acknowledged as a masterpiece, enshrined by the critic Erich Auerbach in his *Mimesis* as one of the standards of realistic literature, of art, following Aristotle's precept, as imitation of "action." Auerbach, however, ultimately finds Stendhal's realism flawed by the very discontinuities—perversities—that make up its greatness for others. Auerbach blames this failure on Stendhal's having been too equally divided between the eighteenth and nineteenth centuries, too torn in both directions to respond completely to either.

Robert M. Adams put his finger on the novel's appeal—or lack of it—by stating that "whether you like Julien Sorel, and for what parts of his behavior, depends, then, in some measure, on who you think you are and what conspiracies or complicities your imagination allows you to join, in the course of reading the book."[8] This sums up the book's genius and its realism, and explains the uniqueness, persistence, and diversity of critical response to it: Julien is a kind of perpetually "floating signifier." Stendhal's realism, as Ann Jefferson points out, is different from that of any other writer because it places "the criterion of realism in the reader and not in the text: 'Un roman est comme un archet [wrote Stendhal], la caisse du violon qui *rend les sons* c'est l'ame du lecteur.' "[9] ("A novel is like a bow; the body of the violin, which makes the sounds, is the soul of the reader" [my translation]).

Such a "performative" realism cannot be accounted for by the same critical strategies deployed to read Balzac or Flaubert or anyone else. For every critic who has scrutinized Stendhal, and *The Red and the Black* in particular, the fiction of Julien Sorel is a special case, a kind of distorting mirror in which the reader may be horrified or pleased to see something of his or her private anxieties and desires against a backdrop of historical circumstances superficially very different from our own, but in some ways quite similar. The paradox of our culture is still that, while the individual may be politically freer than ever before to "pursue" his or her own desires, the power of communities and institutions to police and to manipulate desire, to promote and enforce conformity, has never been greater. As René Girard puts it, "The increasing equality—the approach of the mediator [the individual whose desire we would use as the model of our own] in our terms—does not give rise to harmony but to an even keener rivalry. Although this rivalry is the source of considerable material benefits it also leads to even more considerable spiritual sufferings, for nothing material can appease it. . . . The passion for equality is a madness unequalled except by the contrary and symmetrical passion for inequality, which is even more abstract and contributes even more directly to the unhappiness caused by freedom."[10]

Because of his prophetic sensitivity to this aspect of our modern culture, Stendhal is perhaps more than any other writer of the nineteenth century always ironic and indirect, both in his narrative strategies and in the way he depicts the desire of his characters. Girard, in his *Deceit, Desire, and the Novel,* is not the only critic to have pointed out how the desire of Julien Sorel works never in a straight line but always, with unforeseeable involutions, by a kind of imitative displacement, and thus is always interlarded with ironies (*true* ironies—that is to say, unintended, uncontrolled ones, along with those that are self-aware and intended by a protagonist). By scrutinizing Stendhal's tendency to intrude as author into the narrative of his novels, Victor Brombert has given us in *Stendhal et la voie oblique* an excellent volume on Stendhal's practice of indirection, his penchant for *la voie oblique,* "the indirect way." For Peter Brooks, as for many critics, the irony and the realism of *The Red and the Black* are just as multilayered, ambiguous, and self-displacing as Julien's desires: at once historical, psychological (Freudian), and narratological (structural), the novel remains ironic and even perverse in each of these dimensions considered separately:

> *Le Rouge et le noir,* perhaps more acutely than more "normally" plotted novels, makes us aware of both the consonances and the disjunctures of life and its telling, of event and might-have-been, of biological pattern and concerted deviance from it. [This novel] solicits our attention and frustrates our expectation because we have some sense of the fitting biographical pattern: one in which sons inherit from fathers and pass on, be it through Stephen Dedalus's "apostolic succession," a wisdom gained, a point of understanding attained. Stendhal's perversity may make us realize that such a patterning is both necessary and suspect, the product of an interpretation motivated by desire, and that we also must acknowledge the work of more negative forces of recurrence and revenge.[11]

Such an irony, grounded in the "disjunctures of life and its telling, of event and might-have-been," which ensures that our desire and our pleasure is never quite what we wish it to be, never pure, never even quite real, never entirely our own but at once ours and everyone else's (in magazines and on television), and never entirely *here*, with us, in us, but somewhere else, someone else's first and last and always in our imagination—this kind of irony haunts every one of us, even now, whether we know it or not. This irony gives *The Red and the Black* its compelling plangency, while keeping it from ever becoming sentimental.

Julien's status as " floating signifier" reflects for D. A. Miller a crucial characteristic of Stendhalian realism: its renunciation of closure. Stendhal always tells us too much and not enough; he will not solve the contradictions and mysteries of his character's actions for us.

> What distinguishes Stendhal from these novelists [Jane Austen, George Eliot] is precisely the fact that he elevates this play [narrative suspensiveness, the text's tendency to suspend definitive meanings through the use of irony and ambiguity] (in its full erotic sense) to the position of a supreme value. . . .
>
> The crime [Julien's shooting of Madame de Rênal] anchors the play of meanings in the text, but we are left at sea about the nature of the anchor—always drifting, always restrained by its tug. Julien's act of violence formally puts an end to our anxiety about meaning by giving meaning a location. It also, however, dooms this anxiety to repeat itself in an endless series—endless for the reason that (as Freud said about every search for irreplaceable objects) "every surrogate . . . fails to provide the desired satisfaction." . . . We are set looking, precisely, for an irreplaceable object, the meaning that will regulate and control the novel's production of meaning.[12]

Another aspect of Stendhalian irony to which critics have returned again and again is the discontinuity of time in his work. Georges Poulet put it this way:

> In none of [Stendhal's truly happy moments] is the moment connected with other moments to form a continuous totality of fulfilled existence, as we almost always find it, for instance, in the characters of Flaubert, of Tolstoi, of Thomas Hardy, of Roger Martin du Gard. They all seem, at all times, to carry the full weight of their past (and even of their future destiny) on their shoulders. But the opposite is true of Stendhal's characters. Always living exclusively in their moments, they are entirely free of what does not belong to these moments. Would this mean that they lack an essential dimension, a certain consistency which is the consistency of duration? It could be . . .[13]

Stendhal has no interest in denying that reality as we know it in our lives seldom resembles the kind of straight, continuous lines that make sense, and it never makes *one* sense, but rather many contradictory ones. His "science of happiness" embraced relativity and uncertainty as characteristics of truth long before physics, before Einstein's theory of relativity or Heisenberg's uncertainty principle. A cardinal rule of most realistic fiction, even today, is progression by causality: what a character does must be clearly motivated; what happens to a character must never exceed the reader's sense of what is reasonable and plausible. Character *A* performs act *X*, which has consequences 1, 2, and 3; *A* must then address said consequences, and so on. Implicit in this paradigm are several assumptions, which Stendhal renounces: that the motivations of any individual, including oneself, can be reduced to one definitive understanding; that any act has predictable (plausible) consequences; that everything which happens is the consequence of something which is its "cause"; that it is possible to mean what one says and does, to control precisely the effect of words and deeds on the world around us, to exercise free will unambiguously and to know for sure when one has exercised it.

Stendhal's claimed affinities with logical positivism do not force him to accept any of those assumptions. Logic does not necessarily solve puzzles; indeed, it may make it impossible to solve them. Stendhal shows us characters whom we may pretend to understand only in the partial, myopic, vain, and lopsided ways they see themselves, doing things that they may not entirely want to do but think they want to do, think that they don't want not to do, eliciting consequences that are rarely exactly or only the ones they would have wanted, and confronting events that may be as catastrophic as they are banal and that cannot with certainty be ascribed to any one surely identifiable motivation or cause. Such fictions are rich in comic potential, as Stendhal well knew and did not fail to exploit. It is this aspect of his fiction that has led Ann Jefferson to propose that we view Stendhal's works as *opera buffa*, comic opera. He gives us characters struggling fiercely to assert their will in the face of such a problematic causality, and producing circumstances that are always ambiguous and often absurd, that are at one and the same time the ones desired and yet quite indifferent and dumb and perhaps even opposed to the desire of the protagonist.

Stendhal already knew, as a writer, what deconstructionist criticism is thought to have discovered: that, in the words of Barbara Johnson: "What is undecidable is whether a thing is decidable or not."[14] So we might say that Stendhal was practicing deconstruction before Jacques Derrida had ever invented it. Paul de Man wrote, "It could be argued that the greatest ironists of the nineteenth century generally are not novelists: they often tend toward novelistic forms and devices—one thinks of Kierkegaard, Hoffman, Baudelaire, Mallarmé, or Nietzsche—but they show a prevalent tendency toward aphoristic, rapid, and brief texts (which are incompatible with the duration that is the basis of the novel), as if there were something in the nature of irony that did not allow for sustained movements. *The great and all-important exception is, of course, Stendhal.*"[15]

A Reading

4

A Preface to Reading: On Realism and Mimetic Desire

We live in an age in which the ideology of realism has been so prevalent for so long that everyone takes it for granted and sees it as not an ideology but a fact. An essential part of that ideology is that art defers to reality, imitates reality. In practice, what the ideology of realism has meant is that reality—desire—imitates art, as much as or more than the other way around. This is reality in the sense of an agglomeration of humans and human desires, rather than as Freud defined it, as that which obstructs or inhibits desire.

My morning newspaper today carried the following story, which serves as an example, albeit an extreme one.

(Associated Press) McKee, Ky.—An armed teen-ager apparently acting out the scenario to a Stephen King novel stalked into a high school classroom and took 11 classmates hostage Monday. . . .
The hostage taker was identified by police as Dustin Pierce, a 17-year-old senior at Jackson County High School who was described as a good student. . . .

Stendhal's gravestone in Montmartre cemetery, Paris.

A Preface to Reading: On Realism and Mimetic Desire

> Throughout the daylong negotiations, Stephens [a police detective] said he feared Pierce would try to kill himself since he seemed to be carrying out the scenario of the Stephen King thriller "Rage," which he had been reading.
>
> During a search of Pierce's room at home, police found a paperback copy of the book, in which the lead character is shot by police. The book's plot deals with a youth who holds a classroom of students hostage. . . .
>
> Psychologists and FBI experts who assisted Stephens pored over "Rage" during the day and relayed its details to the negotiators. After reading the book and Pierce's notes, "We thought suicide was what we'd have to deal with at the end," Stephens said.[16]

"Life imitating art" is considered newsworthy only when it leads to some sort of criminal activity. We are all familiar with how John Hinckley was led to an attempt to kill the president by an obsession with the actress Jodie Foster, which began when he saw the film *Taxi Driver,* in which Foster plays a teenage prostitute. I would suggest that in such cases the "abnormality" is not in the fact of imitation but in the extent of it, and in the way in which individuals have (mis)interpreted the "text" in question. We are quite used to the idea of children learning by imitating adults they see on television, and of teenagers duplicating by rote the speech, tastes, mannerisms, and clothing they see on MTV. We do not question the influence of media and celebrities on the public taste—until someone decides to start acting as though life were a movie or a novel in which innocent people get killed. In fact, there are many less violent but nonetheless disturbing instances of this phenomenon happening around us all the time. Stendhal was one of the first novelists to scrutinize this crucial aspect of our mass culture, which probably began, as a mass phenomenon, in the eighteenth century, with the rise of widespread literacy and the emergence of the middle classes as consumers of high and low art.

Because Stendhal is concerned with the way in which the ideology of realism determines our desire, his work is one of social, cultural, and literary theory as well as one of fiction. This is why the narrative contains so many parenthetical "asides," moments in which the narrator, in the manner of the chorus of a Greek drama, seems to step forward and speak directly to the reader. Sometimes these asides are brief; sometimes they go on for a page or longer. Sometimes they merely give us a bit of perspective on a character's knowledge or behavior or understanding, and sometimes they serve the purpose of self-justification, defending the way in which the narrative presents a motif or a character, or articulating an aspect of the ideology of realistic presentation.

These asides are one of the most interesting parts of *The Red and the Black;* without them, it certainly would be a very different novel—though a twentieth-century editor would probably try to excise them as "distractions" from the main current of the story. They are essential to the theoretical purpose of the book, but they also serve a narrative purpose: to engage us as readers in a sort of complicity with the narrator. From a theoretical vantage point, the narrator's reflections on the story he is telling are necessary because of the nature of the story. The kind of desire that is narrated here *cannot see itself directly,* can only be seen playing itself out in the behavior of others, from without. Though describing it and its effects, the narrative voice of the novel cannot exempt itself from those effects any more than we can as readers or as participants in the circuit of desire and the ideology of realism.

In the context of the history of the novel, as I mention in chapter 2, what distinguishes Stendhal from earlier practitioners who were also preoccupied by the way in which desire works and is subject to manipulation, is that he does not believe that such manipulation can be controlled. The act of seduction, even when successful, is subject to ironies—misunderstandings, contingencies—of which the seducer may not even be aware. Often, attempts to seduce or to mislead succeed for reasons entirely different from the ones of which a character may be aware. The ironies of desire, the potential for duplicity within it, can never be definitively contained or avoided.

A Preface to Reading: On Realism and Mimetic Desire

The narrator of Stendhal's novel, and we as well, are engulfed in the same circuit of desire, the same ironies that are visible in the story of Julien Sorel, because the novel itself, literature, the acts of reading and writing, are activities that take place within that circuit of desire. The novel is attempting to do with us, as readers, what Julien would do with the world, to "seduce" us, to make itself appear as a worthy object of our readerly desire, to hold our attention. Books, like people, can hold our attention, our desire, only for as long as we believe that they contain some clues to the secret of happiness. This is a tautology, because it comes down to saying that we can desire only those things (books or people) that are desirable; but it is nonetheless true. The entire system of desire as we know it—of mimetic desire, desire as imitation of other desires; of the ideology of realism, art as *imitation* of something called reality—is generated from that very tautology, or riddle.

5

Leaving Verrières

The Red and the Black, on the surface, observes all the proprieties of an unquestioning realism. It opens like many a realist film, with a panoramic view of the town of Verrières, which, we are told, "is no doubt one of the prettiest small towns in Franche-Comté" (13). Almost as might happen in the opening credit sequence of a television show, we are introduced to the mayor, in whose house Julien will be first employed, apropos of a noise "we cannot help hearing" on entrance into the town: the sound of the mayor's nail factory.

Narration and description proceed in rigorous deference to the model of sensual perception; everything is ordered to seduce us into complicity with the fiction that this is all real, that Verrières is a real town into which we might wander and see and hear and smell just these very things. It is important to recognize this narrative procedure as part of the ideology of realism. What will set Stendhal apart from more run-of-the-mill realists is that he does not take the ideology entirely seriously. On the one hand, the story he tells and the way he tells it appear superficially to show an impeccable respect for the conventional Aristotelian formula of art as a mirror of reality. But on the other hand, Stendhal is also sensitive to the subtle ways in which life imitates art, to the reversals and ironies that make the relation between life and art much more complicated than some practitioners and theorists of realism might pretend.

Apparent coincidence, contingency, appears to structure the book's opening. These "coincidences" are in fact extremely contrived, but do not appear so because they come in the beginning. The entire effect is to make us believe that this could have happened almost anywhere, to anyone—that randomness, not invention, are responsible for the particularities of this place and this story. It is apropos of the mayor, and as a mere aside, that we first hear of Julien's family: "M. de Rênal's gardens, though full of walls, are admired even more because he bought, for their weight in gold, certain small patches of the land they cover. For instance, that sawmill whose odd location on the bank of the Doubs struck you as you came into Verrières, and above which you noticed the name 'SOREL' written in gigantic letters on a sign that rises above the roof—six years ago it occupied the site on which they are now raising the wall for the fourth terrace of M. de Rênal's garden" (15). This introduction to the principal families and their places of business is very much in the manner of Balzac, or almost any other realist of the time. It could be part of the script of a "Masterpiece Theatre" episode now. (The ideology of realism is as intact as ever.) An essential part of the ideology of realism is that all important details appear as though by accident. Pure coincidence, this intersection of families, of individuals, of fates.

Stendhal is playful in his observance of this rule by being so extreme in his obedience to it. In chapter 3 we are introduced not only to the village priest, who has been Julien's Latin teacher and has recommended him as tutor for the mayor's children, but also, through a letter he has written to the priest, to "the Marquis de La Mole, a peer of France and the wealthiest landowner in the province" (20)—Julien's involvement with the La Mole family will follow his stint in the mayor's household. All the significant names are in the first ten pages of the novel.

What sets Stendhal's practice of realism apart is that ironies of coincidence proliferate so unabashedly. By *irony*, I mean a discrepancy between what one character understands and what another does, or between what all the characters understand and what the narrator understands (and what we understand, for we are always, as readers, complicit with the narrator, even if from a distance and to varying degrees). Such irony usually involves misunderstanding, or understanding that occurs by mistake or accident. Often, the stratagems of a character in Stendhal succeed because they are misunderstood, though the character may never know as much, instead assuming that he or she has achieved an end entirely through brilliant machination. Very often, characters make incorrect interpretations or assumptions, misunderstand events or the acts or words or thoughts of others, in a way that in the long run proves quite correct. Julien, for instance, is very pale—so pale that his father had thought "he would not survive" (28)—a prediction that will prove correct by the novel's end, but not on account of his pallor. The motif of a prediction that is ridiculous in its premise, but proves correct quite by accident, is a typical instance of Stendhalian irony.

An even stronger instance occurs a few pages later:

All alone in the church, he [Julien] settled down on the handsomest pew. It bore M. de Rênal's coat of arms. On the kneeling chair, Julien noticed a scrap of printed paper, placed there as if to be read. He glanced at it and saw: "*Details of the last minutes and execution of Louis Jenrel, executed at Besançon, the—*"

The paper was torn. On the other side, he read the first two words of a line, "*The first step—*"

"Who could have put the paper there," Julien wondered. "Poor beggar," he added with a sigh, "his name ends like mine. . . ." And he crumpled the paper.

On his way out, Julien thought he saw blood spilled near the stoup; it was holy water that had been spilled; the reflection of the red

curtains over the windows made it look like blood. Eventually he grew
ashamed of his secret terror. "Shall I be a coward?" he asked himself.
"*To arms!*"
　　This phrase, repeated so often in the old surgeon's accounts of
battles, had a heroic ring for Julien. He got up and walked rapidly toward M. de Rênal's house. (34–35)

Here is a foreshadowing of the novel's and Julien's end. The narrator knows it is such, we suspect it to be such, and so does
Julien. The warning is delivered quite accidentally, by hallucina-
tion (the vision of blood) in concert with happenstance, but this
makes it no less real. Julien accepts his end, and thus his story,
from the beginning, although he does so only half-knowingly.
Most important, the only thing that makes this a warning, and
not a random apprehension, is that this is a novel, and its ending
is already written. Endings lend coherence to random events that
they would not otherwise have; things "signify" that otherwise
could not. Meaning and understanding are always a function of
hindsight, in our own ongoing "stories" as well as finished written ones; in the written stories, however, because their endings
are, from the first page we read, already fixed, we may enjoy an illusion of meaning as unmediated, not dependent on hindsight.
Julien is a bit strange in taking this "omen" so seriously, almost as
though he "knew" he were a character in a novel, where such
small details must always be significant. And indeed, his desire
will always function as the desire to make a story, to behave like a
character in a novel, and so to be one.
　　Highly significant is the way in which we are first introduced
to Julien. We first hear of him before we "see" him, while "eaves-
dropping" on the mayor's plan to hire him as tutor. M. de Rênal's
desire to "uphold our rank" is what makes him wish to have a tutor
knowledgeable in Latin. It is in fact M. de Rênal's desire to appear
grand in everyone's eyes (including his own), his wish to imitate
the desire of others grander than he, who have well-educated tu-
tors for their children—it is this consumerist desire on the mayor's

part that sets Julien's story in motion, that makes everything else possible for Julien. First, we see Julien as an object of desire for someone else (for his knowledge of Latin), not as someone with desires of his own. It is only because the mayor finds him a desirable commodity—one that will bring prestige—that Julien has any opportunity of becoming a "protagonist," of going beyond reading—beyond a vicarious, imaginary, passive participation in the desires of others—to enacting real desires of his own (which will resemble, predictably, the desires he has been reading about, "practicing" in his reading). The mayor gives Julien a chance, the first chance he has had, to be a player rather than a spectator in the drama of power and desire. Because M. de Rênal has the power to "write" Julien into *his* "story," Julien is empowered to attempt to enact the "story" his own desire projects.

What of the stage on which that drama takes place, the town of Verrières itself? It is remarkable not only for its picturesqueness, but also for the pettiness of its citizens, who all—from the mayor to the poorest—have in common the belief that only what "brings in something" (18) has value. Julien, because he hasn't "brought in anything," any revenue, has been thought worthless. But the mayor's desire to be grand will change all that. "The influence of the solid citizen there is, in fact, one of the most irksome kinds of *despotism* imaginable. Because of this wretched word, life in a small town is unbearable for anyone who has lived in that great republic we call Paris. The tyranny of opinion (and what an opinion!) is just as *stupid* in the small towns of France as it is in the United States of America" (16).

Verrières, again in compliance with the ideology of realism which requires that we believe that this story and its locale are not really chosen so much as stumbled upon, is remarkable for its unremarkableness—in spirit, like any small town, in which the tolerance for any sort of exception, any deviation from the norm, is minimal. Here is a paradox of modern culture to which Stendhal will always be sensitive: if our modern age, the age of democracy, of the individual *and* of the empowerment of the masses, increases pressures to conform to one basic paradigm of desire, it does so more the farther we are from the centers of mass urban culture. The same is true today: the cities offer a variety, at least, of modes of conformity, variations on the basic paradigm of desire. But why should we even be concerned with the tyranny of common opinion in the small towns of France at this time—unless we are about to be confronted with an example?

That example follows immediately. We see Julien first *reading a book*—not just any book, but the *Mémorial de Saint-Hélène*, Napoleon's autobiography. Reading, for Julien, is the only mode of participation in life, of enjoyment, of *desire*, available. Language is the only thing he does well. Until now he has only been an object of negative desire (derision, hatred) for others. His slight build and intellectual bent get nothing but contempt from his father, for whom books are a waste of time. His father knocks the book (Julien's favorite) into the river. And only now is the protagonist of the novel described directly, in detail. Our attention is focused on the profound discrepancy between Julien as seen by the mayor, who "desires" him, and as seen by his father, who thinks him useless. The same individual is completely different, opposite, in the eyes of these two individuals. What does this mean? that how a character appears to others has less to do with innate qualities of the individual than with the desires of those around him or her. What appears to us as "reality" is in fact a reflection of our own desire. Stendhal suggests that, while there may indeed be something like an objective, material truth, it means nothing to us until we see in it in relation—positive or negative—to our own desire.

What do we "see" when we look at Julien, at this moment in which he is an object of scorn? Nothing worthy of the narrator's scorn or ours: an attractive but delicate and slight young man who looks younger than he is (19), evidently intelligent and sensitive, but also fiery, with very pale skin and dark chestnut hair, and at times, when angry, a "wicked look." "Looked down upon," nevertheless, "by everyone in the house, he hated his brothers and his father. At the Sunday games on the public square he was always beaten" (28). Still, Julien is "pretty," and the girls have started to notice him—the girls, the mayor, *and the narrator,* and through the latter, *we,* though all for different reasons. He is not only "pretty"; he knows Latin, thanks to an old surgeon major who boarded with the family, gave Julien lessons in Latin and Napoleonic history, and bequeathed him several books and his cross of the Legion of Honor. Since the death of the surgeon, he has taken lessons in theology and Latin from the local priest. So here we have a compelling cipher: a bright, attractive young man, born into a mostly hostile, bigoted milieu. He has two weapons at his disposal: his facility with language (his knowledge of Latin, and knowledge gleaned from a few books) and his looks. These two things, which have only begun to be apparent, will empower him by making him *valuable,* as a real commodity in the story and as a literary commodity to us—capable of "bringing in something" (the only criterion of desirability in our age or his) within the story and as a story. By becoming desirable to others within the narrative in more than a simply negative way, Julien gains an opportunity to enter the game of mimetic desire himself.

He has been waiting for such an opportunity. His desires come from what he has read:

> From his earliest childhood on, he had had moments of exaltation. At such times he would have delightful visions of himself being one day introduced to the beautiful women of Paris; he would attract their attention by some glamorous feat. Why shouldn't he be loved by one of them, as Bonaparte, still a poor man then, had been loved by the dazzling Mme. de Beauharnais? For many years now, scarcely an hour of Julien's life had gone by without his telling himself that Bonaparte, an unknown and penniless lieutenant, had made himself master of the world by his sword. This idea comforted Julien in his misfortunes, which he considered very great, and doubled his joy when joy came to him. (33–34)

This horror of eating with the servants [in M. de Rênal's household] was not instinctive with Julien; in order to make his fortune, he would have done far more disagreeable things than that. He had borrowed this aversion from Rousseau's *Confessions*. It was the only book by which his imagination had formed any idea of society. A collection of the bulletins of the Grand Army and the *Mémorial de Sainte-Hélène* completed his Koran. He would have died for those three works. (30)

Not only would have, but will: another instance of ironic foreshadowing. Julien already has negative, as well as positive, desires, all acquired not through active participation in "life" but from two particular books. All he wishes to know upon learning of his position in the mayor's household is whether he will be obliged to eat with the servants. The comic aspect of this scene is completed by the response of his father, who thinks Julien must be concerned about the quality of the food rather than the company in which it would be eaten. The clash of values could not be clearer. Everyone around him wants money, respects only money and what can be used to get money. Julien cares little for money. His desire is to be an object of desire for others, an object of admiration on a grand scale—someone, like Napoleon, to whom others look in their choice of objects of desire.

This sort of desire—the desire to be looked to as a model, to be an object of positive imitation—as soon as it is recognized as such, is most often judged dangerous in Julien's culture (and in ours, today) to the extent that it has been requited—that it has succeeded in making itself attractive to others, making their desires fix on it as a pattern. Once we realize that someone has sought to manipulate our desire and succeeded in doing so, the former object of our admiration becomes an object of revilement, and will be blamed for that discrepancy in our judgment. The continued success of Julien's desire always depends on not being recognized for what it is. It is always, and remains, the most interesting sort of desire in a culture like ours, in which desire functions by imitation of the desire of others: we want money because someone else has it; we find a woman attractive because someone else, also desirable or admirable, finds her so; a spouse or partner of whom we have grown tired suddenly sparkles with fresh allure because we learn that he or she is desired fiercely by someone else—Stendhal calls such emulative desires "elective affinities"—the title of chapter 7. Julien wants to be a "superstar." When superstars fall from grace, they fall very hard. (The example of Napoleon comes to mind—and we would do well to recall Stendhal's extreme ambivalence about the emperor, as recounted in chapter 1.) It is not accidental that Julien's ambition comes from reading not only Napoleon but also Rousseau. These two figures—Napoleon in politics and Rousseau in literature (in many respects, Rousseau "invented" romanticism)—are arguably the first superstars of modern culture, comparable in their cultural significance to the Beatles or Jackie O. This kind of "megacelebrity" is a distinctly romantic/postromantic phenomenon.

Julien's prodigious memory, and his Latin, make the mayor delighted with his "acquisition" of the boy, and effectively cloak Julien's "desire to be desired," his consuming lust for glory à la Bonaparte. The children adore him, M. de Rênal loves him—all the more because Julien refuses to commit himself to a long-term contract as tutor in the household (no object of desire is ever as dear as the one we cannot be sure of keeping). Julien, however, harbors a "terrible" hatred of everything around him, probably, the narrator tells us, because this society has only barely admitted him: it has not yet placed him where he wishes to be, at the center of everyone else's desire, the object not only of tolerance and mild esteem for his knowledge of Latin, but of positive adulation.

Julien is positively enraged by his own response to Madame de Rênal. He finds her eminently *desirable*, and this gives her a certain power over him that interferes with his desire to be desired (to attain "superstardom," at least locally). Mme. de Rênal is exposed to the spectacle of her maid's unabashed and largely unrequited crush on Julien, which, according to the mimetic structure of

Stendhalian desire, in which desire always chooses objects it has seen chosen by others, cannot help having an influence on her feelings about him, an influence to which she is susceptible because she is too naive to recognize it as such: "Elisa, Mme. de Rênal's chambermaid, had not failed to be smitten by the young tutor; she talked to her mistress about him often" (44). Julien responds by resolving to "seduce" Mme. de Rênal. She, for her part, finds Julien fascinating, and allows herself to find him so because she has not read enough to know that she thus risks falling in love with him:

> In Paris, Julien's relationship with Mme. de Rênal would have been simplified very quickly; but in Paris, love is the child of fiction. The young tutor and his timid mistress would have found their position clarified for them in three or four novels, even in the couplets sung at the *Gymnase*. The novels would have outlined the parts they should play, have shown the model to be imitated; and sooner or later, vanity would have compelled Julien to imitate this model, although with no pleasure and perhaps boggling. (46)

> She [Mme. de Rênal] regarded love, such as she had found it in the few novels chance had put in her way, as exceptional, or even extra-natural. Thanks to her ignorance, Mme. de Rênal was perfectly happy, incessantly concerned about Julien, and far from blaming herself the least bit. (52)

She has no idea what love is, and so is utterly vulnerable to it—the same way that someone totally innocent of what propaganda or advertising are (that is, of their power to manipulate desire) will be utterly susceptible to them.

Julien as seducer succeeds, however, not for the reasons he thinks—not because of any adeptness in his advances—but precisely for the opposite reason: because his gestures seem so awkward to Madame de Rênal, she thinks they must be sincere. His seduction succeeds by failing and thus proceeds as a comedy of misunderstanding. For Julien, there is nothing of pleasure in the seduction. It is rather his duty. He gets such ideas from (where else?) Napoleon:

> Some of things Napoleon says about women, several discussions about the merits of novels that were fashionable during his reign, gave Julien, for the first time in his life, a few of the notions any other young man of his age would have come by long before then. (59)

> . . . Julien considered it part of his *duty* to see to it that this hand [Mme. de Rênal's] should not be withdrawn the next time he touched it. The idea of a duty to be performed, and the ridicule, or rather, the feeling of inferiority to be incurred if he should fail, suddenly drove every pleasurable sensation out of his heart. (60)

> When Julien left Mme. de Rênal's bedroom some hours later, it might be said, in the style of the novel, that he had nothing more to desire. He was, in fact, obliged to the love he had inspired, and to the unexpected impression her seductive charms had made on him, for a conquest that all his clumsy maneuvering could never have brought off.
> Yet, victim of a bizarre pride, even in the sweetest moments he still aspired to the role of a man who is used to subjugating women. He applied himself with incredible effort to spoil whatever was likeable about him. Instead of being attentive to the raptures he had awakened and to the remorse that only heightened their intensity, he could think of nothing but his *duty*. He dreaded the terrible regret and sense of everlasting ridicule that must follow, should he lose sight of the model he had proposed for himself.
> In a word, what made Julien a superior person was precisely what kept him from relishing the happiness that lay at his feet. He was like the sixteen-year-old girl with a lovely complexion who, when she goes to a ball, has the crazy notion of putting rouge on her face.
> . . . In short, nothing would have been wanting to our hero's happiness, not even a burning tenderness in the woman he had just swept off her feet, had he but known how to enjoy it. . . .
> "My God! to be happy, to be loved, is that all there is to it?" Such was Julien's first thought when he got back to his room. He was in that state of astonishment and uneasiness into which a man who has just obtained what he has long desired may lapse. He is used to desiring, has nothing more to desire, and hasn't, as yet, any memories. Like the

soldier who comes back from a parade, Julien was busy reviewing every detail of his conduct.

"Have I failed in any way with respect to what I owe myself? Have I played my part well?"

Which part? That of a man who is used to having his way with women. (95–96)

Julien's view of Madame de Rênal is equally far from her own view of herself, and from the view she thinks that he must have:

"Ah!" she said to herself, "if only I'd met Julien ten years ago, when I was still considered pretty!"

Julien was a long way from thinking like thoughts. He was still in love with ambition. His was the joy of possessing (he, the poor, the wretched, the despised!) such a noble, such a beautiful woman. (99)

Nevertheless, each loves the other "madly," if for different reasons. Julien loves Madame de Rênal because she loves him ("He adored Mme. de Rênal. 'It means nothing to her that she is noble and I a workingman's son; she loves me. . . . For her, I am not a valet who has been assigned the duty of lover'" [124]). For her part, Madame de Rênal loves Julien the more intensely because, with time to reflect upon it, she comes to believe that their affair is a moral crime. This makes the pleasure that she derives from it all the greater. Such are the absurdities of love in our time.

The sense of profound guilt, which whips up her passion to a fever pitch, threatens to make her confess their ongoing "crime" to her husband. Julien is able to defuse this danger, only to have it re-emerge, quite accidentally, at the very same time, from another, totally unforeseen direction:

Mlle. Elisa went to see about a little lawsuit she had going in Verrières. She found M. Valenod very much out of sorts with Julien. She hated the tutor and often talked with M. Valenod about him. . . .

M. Valenod . . . learned a few things that were most mortifying to his vanity.

That woman, the most distinguished in the province, on whom he had lavished so much attention for the past six years, unfortunately in the sight of and to the knowledge of everyone; that proud woman, whose scorn had made him blush so many times, had just taken for her lover a little workingman dressed up as a tutor. To add insult to injury, it appeared that Mme. de Rênal adored her lover. (125)

A thrilling kink thus introduces itself into the web of their desire when M. de Rênal receives an anonymous letter that "exposes" his wife's liaison with his children's tutor. Julien senses something of the sort, and warns Mme. de Rênal. They are saved by the fact, the accident, that he has received other such letters before. Apparently the good citizens amuse themselves with gossip about their mayor's wife, which has always before been groundless. The point of such gossip is not at all to reveal the truth, but to humiliate the mayor. Such is the nature of desire: persons of elevated position, if they are not objects of admiration, become objects of envy or, worse, derision (such are the anxieties of M. Valenod). It is possible, even common, to be all—esteemed, envied, and mocked—at once. The public at large demands certain gestures be made in its favor—for instance, religious and charitable donations, in Monsieur de Rênal's case (he is notoriously cheap in this regard), or in Julien's, the appearance of humility despite his suddenly improved fortunes. If these gestures are not made, admiration tilts in the direction of envy, and vilification in the form of gossip ensues.

The mayor is extremely sensitive to such negative publicity. He does not mind criticism, which is obliged to acknowledge his superiority, but he cannot bear the thought that he might appear ridiculous. If Julien wishes to be everyone's model and object of desire in the grandest sense, to embody their purest and loftiest fantasies, the mayor wishes to be seen as a paragon of everyone's crassest desires, admired for his wealth and station. But no one will want to emulate a cuckold, even a rich and well-connected one. This protects Julien and Madame de Rênal, giving them time to act: the mayor is more concerned with appearing ridiculous than he is with the possibility of his wife's unfaithfulness. "Do not doubt for an instant," Mme. de Rênal tells Julien, "that, as far as you are concerned, my husband will do whatever *public opinion* may prescribe" (129). He feels little real jealousy of his wife, but rather fears appearing a cuckold in the eyes of the public. He would rather not have such an attractive spouse, one capable of inspiring this sort of gossip and giving his "enemies" a weapon of derisive speculation. He has accepted her, and is obliged to keep her, only because of her family's enormous wealth.

Julien and Madame de Rênal embark on an elaborate, mindboggling sequence of feints to convince Monsieur de Rênal that there is nothing going on between them, and that his enemies intend to make him look silly by convincing him of such a thing. He must, then, respond not as though he believed the accusation, but in a way to defuse its potential for making him look foolish. His wife suggests that his principal antagonist, M. Valenod, wishes to hire Julien himself, thus showing up the mayor; in order to do so, he must provoke the tutor's dismissal. The real irony here is that she may be right: M. de Valenod does wish to take Julien away from the mayor's employ, and he might have authored the anonymous letter for this reason, seeking to turn events to his advantage rather than simply to appease his jealous rage—if indeed M. Valenod is the author of the letter at all; we never know for certain.

In fact, it makes no difference who the letter came from or what motivated it. What an individual may intend, or *mean*, counts for little in this game of desire. The only thing that matters is how the *sign*, the representation of intention, plays in the minds of those who receive it. Attempts to control the message's reception, its meaning, by framing it with other messages, may or may not work, for any additional messages will function in the same way, their import usually determined more by accident—by the messages, signs, that happen to frame them in turn—than anything else. Often the messages we didn't intend do more to save us (or destroy us) than the ones we give out deliberately. The machinations in which Julien and his lover engage to throw M. de Rênal and the citizens of Verrières off their scent are both hilarious and plausible. They take such pleasure in the ruse that it becomes an end in itself without their realizing it. The purpose of the whole undertaking is to allow them to go on undetected with their affair; the end result is to end the affair just as effectively as if the mayor had believed the letter sent to him: Julien is sent by the mayor to study at the seminary in Besançon.

Perhaps most significant for Julien at this point in the story is that he has become sufficiently important in the eyes of the public to figure as a protagonist in their everyday narratives (gossip), an object no longer of derision but rather of indignant envy and resentment, and only when he makes the correct gestures of humility and "goodness," of unadulterated admiration. He learns, from this episode, that he must play to a larger audience than he had at first realized.

> The great misfortune of small towns in France, and of governments by election, like that of New York, is that you are never allowed to forget that fellows like M. de Rênal exist in the world. In the midst of a city of twenty thousand inhabitants such individuals mold public opinion, and public opinion is a terrible thing in a country that has a constitution. A man endowed with a noble and generous mind, and who might have been your friend but lives a hundred leagues away, judges you according to public opinion in your town, which is shaped by the fools whom chance has caused to be born noble, rich, and conservative. Woe to anyone who stands out from the crowd! (155)

Equally important is that Julien's conspiracy with Madame de Rênal fails by succeeding: it effectively ends their affair. It serves the purposes of Monsieur de Rênal quite as well as he could wish. By being duped utterly, he may be more effectively protected from the designs of his enemies and from ridicule than he ever could have made himself on purpose.

At the seminary, Julien learns another valuable lesson about the way the desire of one's "public" works, or at least we do. It is really the same lesson he got as an object of gossip back in Verrières: that he must remember that he is playing seducer to many, not just one or two, to those behind, around, and below as well as above. His tendency to forget this will be his downfall, as perhaps it might be for anyone with the same sort of ambition; sooner or later, a miscalculation is bound to occur. The lesson is that excellence, talent, merit, in themselves do not inspire love. Unless they are tempered just so by the right gestures of seduction—the appearance of humility, of goodness, of not posing a threat to anyone—they will do quite the opposite, provoking hatred (the nasty face of desire) rather than affection.

> Julien thought he might be able to turn M. de Maistre's book *Du Pape* to his advantage. To tell the truth, he astonished his companions; but this was another piece of bad luck. He offended them by setting forth their own opinions better than they could. M. Chélan had been as reckless with regard to Julien as he had been on his own account. After having instilled in him the habit of close reasoning and of not allowing himself to be satisfied with idle chatter, he had neglected to tell him that in a person of no consequence this habit is a crime; for sound reasoning always offends.
>
> Julien's gift of gab was, therefore, a fresh crime against him. By dint of thinking about him, his companions succeeded in expressing all the horror he inspired in them with two words; they nicknamed him Martin Luther. (193–94)

Julien is in grave danger, just as the mayor was, of appearing ridiculous. He is saved, as always, by having so effectively seduced those above him, if not those below.

The name of the Marquis de La Mole, which has been occurring regularly up to this point, now emerges as Julien's ticket to the really grand stage of desire, Paris. The Abbé Pirard, director of the seminary, secures him the position of secretary to the Marquis, warning the latter that Julien will perform well only so long as his pride is not wounded by being treated as a servant. The Marquis assures him that this will not be a problem. He will make Julien the companion of his son (218).

Julien makes a farewell visit to his former co-conspirator, Madame de Rênal, only to find that she has completely repented of her infatuation with him. It takes three hours for him to reseduce her. That seduction, like their concerted deception of M. de Rênal, is mostly a matter of deploying language in an effective manner, constructing a narrative into which Mme. de Rênal will feel her desire to be drawn, inexorably though suddenly. His success is signaled precisely by a linguistic sign in her language, a change from the formal *vous* to the familiar *tu* in her address, by which she assents to her place in the "story" of desires (his and hers) that Julien is narrating.

> Seated beside the woman he adored, almost holding her in his arms, in the room where he had been so happy, in the midst of profound darkness, distinguishing clearly that for the last few minutes she had been weeping, realizing, from the heaving of her breast, that she was holding back her sobs, he had the bad luck to become a cold politician, almost as calculating and cold as when, in the courtyard of the seminary, he saw himself exposed to some malicious prank by a companion stronger than he. Julien stretched his story and went on talking about the unhappy life he had led since his departure from Verrières.
>
> . . . Julien saw that his story was a success. He realized that it was now time to play his last card: he came abruptly to the letter he had just received from Paris. . . .
>
> "You are going to Paris!" cried Mme. de Rênal rather loudly. [Here, at last, she suddenly reverts to calling Julien by the familiar *tu*] . . .
>
> "Yes, madam, I am leaving you forever. I hope you will be happy. Farewell."
>
> He took the few steps to the window; he was already opening it. Mme. de Rênal sprang toward him. He felt her head on his shoulder and himself being clasped in her arms as she pressed her cheek against him.
>
> Thus, after three hours of dialogue, Julien obtained that which he had desired so passionately during the first two. Coming a bit sooner, this reversion to tender feelings, the disappearance of Mme. de Rênal's

remorse, would have meant divine happiness; thus obtained, by art, it was nothing more than a triumph. (225–26)

Her love is restored in all its violence by the news that he is leaving for Paris. While at Besançon, she had thought of him as a "possession" that she did not risk losing, securely locked up in his seminary like a canary in a cage. Her desire had starved nearly to death without either physical or metaphysical food, without his presence or the threat of losing him. As Proust would put it, "the only real paradises are the ones that have been lost"—or that threaten to be lost.

Julien exits the first half of the novel, exits Verrières, ignominiously: taken for a burglar (his liaison with Madame saved again from exposure by an accidental misunderstanding), he is chased naked from the mayor's estate, a hail of bullets following him.

6

In the Hôtel de
La Mole

Julien's desire, as we observed already, is unlike most people's. His desire is to be a superstar on the order of Napoleon or Rousseau, an object, and a model, for the desire of others. This makes his desire different because it has as its object the desires of others; he desires to occupy a particular place in the circuit of mass desire. There is an element of this sort of desire in all of us: we all want to be liked, even admired. Julien, however, wants it on a very grand scale, and wants nothing else. Just as Napoleon and Rousseau, or rather the stories of their desire, have become models for his desire, so Julien wishes to *become a story* that will compel the desires of others. He needs particular objects of desire—women, material advancement—in order to make such a story. These, however, are secondary for Julien, whereas they would be primary for most people.

The ideal sort of woman for Julien to make his story with would be one whose desire would dovetail perfectly with his. What would such a desire be like? It would have to be a desire to figure in a story like Julien's: to act the part of "object of desire" in a narrative of superstardom, to play Josephine to someone's Napoleon.

This desire is to be a superstar by being a superstar's "great love." It differs from an ordinary desire to be loved by a man because it desires a very particular sort of man: not only one who wants to be "famous" or "glorious" or "powerful" and promises to be, but one who wishes to attain these adjectives in such an unorthodox yet "fashionable" and compelling way as to fire the imaginations of the public, of such young men as Julien Sorel.

In the second part of *The Red and the Black*, Julien (of course) encounters just such a young woman in the person of Mathilde de La Mole. Mathilde is fascinated by history just as Julien is, but history of more remote vintage. A discrepancy in historical backdrop will not, however, prevent their fantasies from being spliced together without a seam. Julien, because he is odd in the context of Parisian society, and because of the way he is odd, seems "historical" to Mathilde and to others. He seems to belong in the history books more than in real Paris:

> "O heavens! could he be another Danton?" Mathilde asked herself. "But he has such a noble face, and Danton was so horribly ugly, a butcher, I think." (295)

> "Watch out for that young man who is so energetic," her brother warned. "If the revolution flares up again, he will have us all guillotined." (315)

> Ah! [Mathilde says to herself] in the heroic age of France, in Boniface de La Mole's day, Julien would have been the major, and my brother the young priest with the right ideas, with caution in his eyes and reason on his tongue. (329–30)

This happens despite Julien's awe of the place and of the nobility, and despite the great potential for him to appear ridiculous rather than admirable.

Upon entering the Marquis's service (and the second part of the novel), Julien notices that he is surrounded by all sorts of "stories," texts resplendent in their bindings: once accepted here, a "story" like Napoleon's would be far grander, more exalted than it ever could have been in the household of M. de Rênal, who had no such "library":

> So as not to be observed in his excited state, he went and hid himself in a gloomy little corner; from there he gazed rapturously at the shining backs of the books. "I will be able to read all of them," he told himself. . . .
>
> Julien ventured over to the books; he went almost mad with joy on finding an edition of Voltaire. He ran and opened the library door so as not to be caught in the act. Next he gave himself the pleasure of opening each of the eighty volumes. They were magnificently bound, the masterpiece of the best binder in London. (248)

The library is a metaphor for the grander, larger milieu of Parisian nobility, and the books it contains—far more numerous and beautiful than any Julien has seen before—are all narrative models of desire, consecrated by printing and binding, which Julien, by his own narrative, his own example, seeks to exceed and supersede.

But language here is a trickier medium than it was in the provinces. Julien misspells the word *cela* on his first day, writing it with two *l*s: *cella*. His Latin saves him, just as always. A "dead" language, it, like Julien, can mean all things to all people. It signifies learning, erudition, sophistication, elevation, to all audiences, whether the crude, money-grubbing bourgeois or the wealthy nobility. Behind Latin, Julien can conceal his origins, his admiration of Napoleon, and the nature of his desire. Latin is a kind of "magic powder" that enables Julien's disadvantages to become invisible, raising him above whatever milieu he finds himself in. Working from the cover of Latin, Julien quickly masters the nuances of this more sophisticated social language.

He learns, for instance, that in order to avoid the possibility of embarrassment, one must always "do the contrary of what is expected of you," as Prince Korasoff tells him in chapter 24 of part 2 (281). The marquis tells the story of Julien's bad spelling to everyone at dinner that night; when Julien ignominiously falls off his horse riding with the marquis's son, he is quick to tell the story himself. This throws everyone, particularly Mathilde, off guard:

> "Monsieur le Comte is too good to me; I thank him and am deeply appreciative. He was kind enough to give me the gentlest and the best-looking horse; but after all, he couldn't fasten me to it, and for lack of that precaution, I had a fall in the middle of that long street near the bridge."
>
> Mlle. Mathilde tried in vain to smother a burst of laughter; then tactlessly she asked for details. Julien acquitted himself with a good deal of naturalness; he had style without knowing it. (254)

What can this be? A young man unconcerned about appearing ridiculous? Why, then he must be extraordinary. Julien wears an apparent contempt for the aristocracy around him, despite his humble origins and his awe on first arriving in the marquis's household. This haughtiness, together with his awkwardness, makes Julien appear *different* to all the jaded aristocrats, bored with each other. He positively fascinates everyone, and because he acts in every way contrary to their expectations—to what they would expect of a provincial like Julien—everyone is quick to interpret his ignorance and awkwardness as signs of a superior temperament and intellect:

> "The awkward manners of this young abbé may well hide a learned man," said the academician, seated next to the marquise. . . . Stock phrases suited the mistress of the house's turn of mind very well; she adopted this one about Julien and congratulated herself on having invited the academician to dine. (252)

> "Despite the disadvantages of his eternal black outfit and of his priestly ways, which he certainly must keep up, poor boy, or risk starving to death, his ability frightens them; nothing could be plainer. . . . whenever one of those gentlemen says something he considers clever and unexpected, doesn't he always look at Julien first? . . . Well, my father, a superior man who will add greatly to the fortune of our house, respects Julien. Everyone else hates him, but no one is contemptuous of

him, except my mother's sanctimonious lady friends" [Mathilde says all this to herself]. (316)

The depth, the *unknown quantity* of Julien's character might have frightened her even if she were establishing an ordinary relation with him. (330)

Rather like Chance, the protagonist/antihero of Jerzy Kosinski's novel *Being There* (and the film of the same name)—an illiterate gardener who is misinterpreted as Chauncey Gardner, wealthy confidant of presidents—Julien's faults are (accidentally, and erroneously) read as virtues because they do not look like faults are supposed to look in upper class Parisian society. " 'You are predestined, my dear Sorel,' they told him. 'That cold look of being *a thousand leagues away from the present stir*, which we try so hard to assume ourselves, comes naturally to you' " (281).

Julien thus accomplishes his wish of becoming a center of attention partly by design but mostly by accident. By telling everyone of his fall from the horse, he negates the possibility of Norbert telling everyone as the marquis had told them of his poor spelling. By appearing contemptuous of aristocratic society, he conceals his ignorance of its subtleties.

Mathilde is sick to death of the young men of her social rank—ripe, thus, for casting Julien in her private fantasies: "It was her misfortune to be more intelligent than MM. de Croisenois, de Caylus, de Luz, and her other gentlemen friends. She could imagine everything they would say to her" (286). The young male nobles are all the same, too "perfect" in their homogeneity, "all pale copies of one another" (357): " 'It's no use; I could never love Croisenois, Caylus, and *tutti quanti*. They are perfect, too perfect, perhaps; in a word, they bore me' " (312). "The more they bantered gracefully about everyone who was out of step with the fashion, or followed it awkwardly, under the impression of keeping up with it, the lower they sank in her estimation" (329).

Here we see the paradox that governs mass culture: it makes

everyone the same by making everyone want to be different (and believe that he or she is different); Mathilde de La Mole says to herself. " 'Everything about the destiny of a girl like me ought to be unusual' " (330). Mimetic desire enforces conformity by championing the individual. Everyone wishes to be a special case, and those we admire are, by definition, seen as "special," extraordinary, exceptional. Yet everyone tends to be more or less the same because everyone tends to admire the same examples, to pattern his or her desire after the same models. Still, heroes survive as such only as long as we can believe in them as exceptions. The ideal hero would be one whom no one else knows about—who is "ours alone"—and yet whom we know would be everyone else's if they knew about him or her, or weren't stupid and tasteless. The "urtext," the narrative model of Mathilde's desire, is given to us very explicitly:

> On the thirtieth of April, 1574, the best-looking boy of his day, Boniface de La Mole, and his friend Annibal de Coconasso, a Piedmontese gentleman, had their heads cut off on the Place de Grève. La Mole was the adored lover of Queen Marguerite de Navarre. "Note," added the academician, "that Mlle. de La Mole is named *Mathilde-Marguerite*. La Mole was, at the same time, the Duke d'Alençon's favorite and the intimate friend of the King of Navarre, afterward Henry IV, his mistress's husband. On Mardi Gras of that year 1574, the court was at Saint-Germain with poor King Charles IX, who was dying. La Mole tried to carry off the princes, his friends, whom the queen, Catherine de' Medici, had detained at court as prisoners. He brought up two hundred horsemen beneath the walls of Saint-Germain; the Duke d'Alençon lost his nerve, and La Mole was thrown to the headsmen.
>
> "But the thing that touches Mlle. Mathilde—she told me so herself, some seven or eight years ago, when she was twelve, for she has a head! a head! . . ." And the academician rolled his eyes heavenward. "The thing that struck her most in this political catastrophe is that Queen Marguerite de Navarre, hidden in a house on the Place de Grève, dared to send someone to ask the executioner for her lover's head. And the following night, at midnight, she took that head in her carriage and

went and buried it herself in a chapel situated at the foot of the hill of Montmartre."

"Is it possible?" cried Julien, deeply touched.

"Mlle. de La Mole despises her brother because, as you can see, he doesn't give a rap for all that ancient history and never wears mourning on April thirtieth." (304)

Note the way in which the "academician" serves very much the same purpose within the story as a real scholar would by annotating the text of *The Red and the Black*: he "annotates" the "texts" of the other characters' behavior; the novel thus contains not only a main character who wishes to be the protagonist of a *romanesque* (in French, both romantic and novelistic) narrative and calculates (or tries to) his every word and action accordingly, but also its own "scholarly annotator." The key to understanding any character, and indeed any person, is to find the story that structures their desire. Thanks to the academician, we know that Boniface de La Mole is Mathilde's favorite "superstar." His story is not the only one she likes, though. She is more than narcissistic enough to prefer narratives in which a strong female protagonist figures: "One day she related to him, her eyes aglow with pleasure, which proved the sincerity of her admiration, the deed of a young woman who lived during the reign of Henry III, about which she had just read in l'Etoile's *Mémoires*. Discovering that her husband was unfaithful, she stabbed him" (305).

The best stories are like those of Marguerite de Navarre, in which a "star" like Boniface de La Mole is destroyed and consecrated at the same time by an act of heroic iconoclasm, and his lover survives to build a cult around him. Who could make a better Boniface than Julien? The picture in her mind's eye of Boniface, her ideal imaginary object of desire, starts to fuse with images of Julien Sorel: "Mathilde . . . kept sketching haphazardly on a page of her album. One of the profiles she had just finished amazed, delighted her: it bore a striking resemblance to Julien. 'This is the voice of heaven! Here is one of love's miracles,' she said to herself ecstatically. 'Unwittingly I have drawn his portrait' " (357). Unwittingly, the narrative of her desire happens to find just the place for Julien that he would wish to occupy, according to the narrative exigencies of his own.

Perhaps the worst thing about this kind of desire—Julien's and Mathilde's, and everybody's to some degree—is that the only pleasure that seems real and complete to it is that which is experienced vicariously: read about, seen, imagined, or remembered. Count Altamira says as much to Julien:

> "There are no genuine passions left in the nineteenth century; that is why everyone is so bored in France. People commit the greatest cruelties without cruelty. . . .
>
> "Every act is performed without pleasure and without recollection, even crimes." (297)

> "That is because your antiquated society prizes conformity above everything else. . . . It can never rise above military courage; you will have your Murats but never a Washington. I see nothing in France but vanity. The man who finds his ideas as he is speaking may very well happen to make an ill-advised remark, but if he does, the master of the house considers himself disgraced." (299)

Any desire that does not imitate prevalent models of desire in its choice of objects and its expression is considered at best uncouth and at worst scandalous, criminal. Everyone's desire is quite unreal to him or her, or not as real as the model of desire that inspired it. The circuit of desire is never completed in the present, here, but always at another time in history or another place, in the "story" of someone else, on the football field or in Paris or Hollywood or New York; desire no longer seeks requital directly, but rather the spectacle of requital (which is often scandalous; the *National Enquirer*, for instance, like many other tabloid publications, panders directly to the public's obsession with vicarious desire, desire as spectacle), the story or image of it; pleasure is not something we experience directly as much as something we see on television,

read about in books or magazines, something in which we partici-
pate vicariously. "Real life" is always happening somewhere else
than our living room: past the TV screen, the movie screen, in the
pages of books. This means that there is no reality at all: reality is an
idea, a fantasy—the ultimate fantasy, the greatest novel of all,
which is still being "written."

In order for anyone to experience pleasure of any sort, to any
degree, there must be either total vicariousness, total deference to
desire as spectacle (so that pleasure is entirely in watching) or some
sort of fusion of watching and doing: this would be a repetition, an
imitation of a model that is somehow also immediate and original,
that is itself a model—a spectacle of desire for others. The latter is
what Julien and Mathilde de La Mole aim for. They wish to enact
their own spectacle while modeling it after others (Napoleon,
Rousseau, Boniface de La Mole). But this kind of pleasure is not
immediate; it has mediation built into it, because it tries to be two
things at once: it looks to its audience, in seeking to be a "spectacle
of desire" for others, and it looks to its own models, as an audience. Julien is at one point tempted by the idea of suicide (at a low
moment, when he believes that Mathilde prefers some "young offi-
cer" to him), but decides against it not because he fears death, or
decides that he has things yet to live for, but because it would not
make Mlle. de La Mole think any better of him.

Stendhal calls this way of looking at oneself (Julien's and
Mathilde's) *inverted imagination*: the attempt to imagine how we
look in the eyes of others. Inverted, because it not only seeks to see
inside the thoughts of others, but to look back at itself through the
eyes of others.

> "And in fact, I'm not worth much!" Julien told himself, fully convinced,
> "on the whole, I am a very dull fellow, very common, very boring to
> others, unbearable to myself." He was sick to death of all his good qual-
> ities, of everything he had once cared for enthusiastically; and in this
> state of *inverted imagination*, he undertook to judge life with his
> imagination. . . .

In the Hôtel de La Mole

The idea of suicide occurred to him several times....

"My death will make her even more contemptuous of me!" he cried. "What a memory I shall leave!" (360)

This is very strange. Death in itself seems like "a charming notion" (360), but Julien holds back from it because it must come in the right way, at the right time; it must make the right impression. Important to note is that he always takes death—the right death, at the right moment—as the proper end to his story. He thinks of himself as though that ending had already been written, as we know it has. " 'I mustn't do anything, not say anything today,' he thought on coming back to the house,'—be as dead physically as I am spiritually. Julien is no more; it is my corpse that moves' " (364). " 'I'm a corpse,' " he tells his friend Prince Korasoff (395).

The irony of such moments, the fact that Julien does not realize how true these statements are, only serves to underscore them. They hark back to his father's prognostication that the boy would not live long, inspired (wrongly) by his paleness. It is as though he knew himself to be the protagonist of a novel whose bloody ending has already been written, all of whose scenes must be contrived to set that ending in the best light. All pleasure is subordinated to that "end."

Even when the act is sexual, the pleasure is an odd, bloodless one. The scene of Julien's and Mathilde's mutual "seduction" is far more awkward than the earlier, similar one involving Mme. de Rênal. This is true because both Julien and Mathilde are acting. Mme. de Rênal, at least, had been too naive to calculate when Julien first slept with her; this had saved the moment for both of them.

Julien was embarrassed; he didn't know how to act; he felt no love at all. In his confusion, he thought he should be forward; he tried to kiss Mathilde.

"Shame on you!" she said, pushing him away. (340)

He resorted to his memory, as once before long ago in Besançon with Amanda Binet, and recited several of the most beautiful passages in the *Nouvelle Héloïse*.

61

"You have a man's heart," she answered, without listening very closely to his recitation. . . .

Mathilde was making an effort to address him familiarly, and she was obviously more attentive to this odd manner of speech than to the sense of what she was saying. (342)

To tell the truth, their raptures were a bit forced. For them, passionate love was still a model to be imitated rather than a reality. (343)

If there was no tenderness in his heart, it was because Mathilde, in all her behavior with him, however strange it may sound, had been fulfilling a duty. There had been nothing unexpected for her in all the events of that night, except the wretchedness and shame she experienced, instead of that heavenly bliss of which the novels speak. (344)

The jarring discrepancy between this very physical, immediate, sexual act, and the vicarious pleasure of desire as spectacle, disconnects Julien from the circuit of Mathilde's desire. Her physical, tactile experience of Julien separates him from the Julien of her imagination, from Boniface de La Mole, from all idealized stories of love. To reconnect the two narratives of their desire, Julien must now engage in a series of feints almost perfectly like the ones in which he and Mme. de Rênal engaged to defuse the letter sent to M. de Rênal. Julien consults his friend Korasoff, who advises him to act as though he desires another woman in order to resuscitate Mathilde's passion through jealousy. Korasoff gives Julien a whole stack of "real" love letters which he is to copy in his own hand and send to this pretended object of his desire. Julien even forgets to change the names of cities in copying one of the letters. The following comic moment ensues:

"How does it happen," she [Mme. de Fervaques] asked him the next day, with an air of indifference, which he found poorly played, "that you speak to me of *London* and of *Richmond* in a letter you wrote last night, so it seems, after coming out of the opera?"

Julien was quite embarrassed; he had copied line for line without a thought to what he was writing, and had obviously forgotten to substitute *Paris* and *St. Cloud* for *London* and *Richmond* in the original. He began two or three sentences with no possibility of finishing them; he felt himself on the verge of giving in to a giggle. At last, while hunting for his words, he came upon this idea: "Uplifted by the most sublime of discussions about the greatest of concerns of the human soul, my mind, as I wrote you, may well have wandered." (413)

The effect of such letters has little or nothing to do with what they say; they are even more effective because they strike Mme. de Fervaques as so completely unlike Julien:

> It was the contrast between the apparent frivolity of his conversation and the sublime and almost apocalyptic depth of his letters that had distinguished him. The widow especially liked the length of his sentences; "this isn't the choppy style made fashionable by Voltaire, that immoral man!" (413)

> Little by little she took the pleasant habit of writing almost every day. Julien would answer with faithful copies of the Russian letters and, such is the advantage of the high-flown style, Mme. de Fervaques was not in the least surprised that there was so little connection between his replies and her letters. (417)

What is at stake in such a written exchange, Stendhal seems to imply, is not the content of the letters, what they "mean"—for they mean little or nothing in themselves—but rather the effect produced by the letters. In a different novel, by a different author, Julien's success at manipulating Mathilde in this way, by jealousy, might be expected to depend upon how convincingly sincere his desire for the other woman appears. In fact, Julien's insincerity is not only apparent to Mathilde, but makes him appear all the more desirable.

When she discovers a drawerful of letters to Julien from Mme. de Fervaques which he has not even opened, Mathilde exclaims " 'So . . . not only are you on good terms with her, you despise her as well. You, a nobody, to scorn the Field Marshall de Fervaques' widow!' " (419). Julien has not opened the letters because he does not care what they say. He ought in fact to have opened them, in order to give the appearance of caring, but not having opened them, as it turns out, quite accidentally impresses Mathilde even more—or she pretends that it does, since she notices that the letters are addressed in Julien's handwriting, not Mme. de Fervaques's (the latter perversely insists that Julien prepare "self-addressed envelopes" for her replies to his copied letters because of the "unseemliness of writing such a commonplace address in her own hand" [417]).

Mathilde may (must?) think that the letters are some sort of sham to make her think that Mme. de Fervaques is writing to Julien, because the novel tells us "she gave a nervous, quite noticeable start when she recognized the widow's writing" (420). She seems, indeed, to understand Julien's relations with the widow as a sham altogether, and yet she is quite as effectively manipulated as if she did not. She admires the spectacle of his "falseness," of his deceitfulness in the effort to make her jealous. "What astonished her the most was his perfect falseness; he never said a word to the widow but it was a lie, or at least an abominable disguise for his true opinion, which Mathilde knew perfectly well on almost every subject. His Machiavellianism impressed her. 'Such depth!' she would tell herself. 'What a difference between him and the pompous boobies or common crooks, such as M. Tanbeau, who talk the same language!' " (414).

When she decides that she does love Julien after all, Mathilde reassumes her place in the circuit of his desire by pretending that all his feinted desire for another has made her jealous as it is supposed to have. She allows Julien—and herself—to believe that his feint has succeeded. And it has, but only by being recognized by her as feint, not, as Julien thinks, by having been misunderstood as real. Even when she knows the letters from Mme. de Fervaques to be authentic, despite Julien's handwriting on the outside of them, she only pretends to read them. Mathilde is jealous not of Julien's affections but of his falseness, because she knows that his falseness is the purest expression of his desire. The multiple layers of misunderstanding and lucidity, of pretense and counterpretense and counter-counterpretense—copied letters representing feigned love, unopened letters mistakenly assumed to be counterfeit and then not read anyway—are enough to make us dizzy. Once again, Julien's efforts to gain someone's affections succeed for the wrong reasons.

But they do succeed. Julien demands a proof of her love from Mathilde, and she agrees to give it to him. She will become pregnant by him, and thus disgraced in the eyes of her family and class. This will make her utterly dependent on Julien, his "slave." Her father, learning that she is pregnant, makes the best of things by getting Julien appointed a lieutenant in the Hussards and buying him a noble title (Julien Sorel de la Vernaye). At this point the story seems to be winding toward a "happy" ending, one typical of an English Victorian novel by Dickens or George Eliot. Even Julien begins to experience much more homely instincts than he ever has before, abandoning all notions of superstardom in favor of a vision of familial bliss. All his thoughts are for his future son. " 'After all,' he [Julien] thought, 'my novel is finished, and the credit is due to me alone. I was able to make that monster of pride fall in love with me,' he added, looking at Mathilde. 'Her father can't live without her, nor she without me' " (446).

Note, though, that the pleasure here is still a pleasure in having successfully manipulated the desires of others. It is not a simple, unmediated bliss, though it wishes to masquerade as one, and now, perhaps, even to become one. Stendhal's novel suggests that, in a world in which desire works by imitation, there can be no such thing as an unmediated happiness. Desire is always enacted at a distance, through the eyes of those who are its spectators and by repeating the desires of others. The Victorian ideal of true love, marriage, and the homely pleasures of family is one more ethereal spectacle of desire—the one we see represented on television as "The Ozzie and Harriet Show" or "Mayberry RFD"—which we can experience only as Julien does, as something to be approximated, an idea, not an immediate reality we know through experience, but one we take pleasure in resembling, in believing.

This explains the extraordinary public demand for such representations, in Stendhal's time and in our own, and it also explains why *The Red and the Black* was so hard to swallow for so many people. It has a perfect opportunity to give us this representation of the "happy ending," of the triumph—despite Julien's and Mathilde's and everyone else's cynicism—of homely pieties. But that is not the ending we get. For Julien to sustain that illusion plausibly would require a perfect manipulation of everyone's desire, not just the desires of Mathilde and her father, and of course his own. And Julien is no longer in a position to manipulate Mme. de Rênal's desire. He has even forgotten that he needs to. The Marquis solicits information about Julien's past from Mme. de Rênal, urged to do so by "the shameless man himself" (450). She denounces him as a ruthless and cynical seducer—an ironic response, when we recall that Julien's maladroitness was what had charmed her most.

Julien's response is perhaps the closest he has or will come to unpremeditated action, action without any thought of consequences or of what others might think: he buys a gun and tries to kill Madame de Rênal while she is attending mass.

Our chance for a "happy ending" is ruined. And this is what makes *The Red and the Black* a "scandalous" book. It would have had to betray itself completely, however, to end any way but the way it does. Stendhal has already pointed out the implicit scandalousness of one of his main characters and, by inference, of his entire narrative. He has undertaken to show in the novel itself the way in which novels and other models of desire work, the way in which reality imitates representations of reality, and desire imitates other desires. Inasmuch as novels are very much part of this circuit of desire, Stendhal has broken the rules. He has written a narrative that, while participating in the circuit of desire by appealing to our readerly desire, constitutes an exposé of itself and us, of the game of mimetic desire in which we are all subsumed. If our pleasure in the trick is at all dependent on believing that there is no trick, but rather actual magic, if we have any desire invested in believing that our desire is unmediated by imitation and that reality exists independently of the stories we tell ourselves and each other about it, then we are bound to be offended, scandalized. What Stendhal does here is analogous to an adult dressing up in a Santa Claus suit in order to tell a child that there is no Santa Claus—there isn't one, but let's act as though there were because that's fun too. There is also "fun" in the knowledge that we are engaged in an illusion, fun in knowing how it works, but this is a highly intellectual kind of pleasure, and not to everyone's taste.

His defense of the character of Mathilde de La Mole, in which Stendhal brazenly contradicts himself, shows us just how amused his narrative is by the conventions that govern it. The novel cannot escape those conventions, any more than we can escape the conventions imposed upon us by our profession or community or laws, but we may attain a certain distance, a passive autonomy and even superiority by understanding how those conventions work. Their power over us is far greater without such understanding, for without it, we cannot see the narrative structures that determine us; we accept them as more real and natural than ourselves.

(This page will harm the poor author in more ways than one. Frigid hearts will accuse him of indecency. Yet he would not do the young people who shine in Parisian drawing rooms the injustice of supposing that anyone among them is susceptible to the mad impulses that are undermining Mathilde's character. That character is altogether imaginary and, in fact, imagined well outside the pale of those social customs which guarantee so distinguished a place among all the centuries to the civilization of the nineteenth.

It is not prudence that was wanting in the girls who were the ornament of the balls last winter.

Nor do I think one can rightly accuse them of being overly contemptuous of a brilliant fortune, horses, fine estates, and all those

things which assure a woman an agreeable position in society. Far from
being bored by all those advantages, they generally make them the object of their most constant desires, and if there is any passion in their
hearts, it is for such things.

Nor is it love that guides the careers of young men endowed with
some talent, like Julien; they fasten themselves to a coterie with an in-
vincible grip, and when the coterie comes into its own, all the good
things of society rain down upon them. Woe to the intellectual who is
not allied to a clique; even his smallest, most dubious success will at-
tract nothing but blame, and lofty virtue will triumph in the act of
robbing him. Well, sir, a novel is a mirror being carried down a highway. Sometimes it reflects the azure heavens to your view; sometimes,
the slime in the puddles along the road. And you will accuse the man
who carries the mirror on his back of immorality! His mirror shows you
slime, and you blame the mirror! Rather, blame the highway where the
puddles stand; or rather still, blame the inspector of roads who allows
the water to stagnate and the puddles to form.

Now that we are agreed that Mathilde's character is impossible in
our time, an age no less prudent than virtuous, I will be less concerned
about provoking the reader as I get on with my story of that lovable
girl's follies.) (358–59)

According to the conventions, the ideology of mimetic realism, the characters and events of the novel must defer to truth, to
the real, by admitting their distance from it. They must resemble
the truth but not usurp its metaphysical primacy. Stendhal uses and
threatens the convention by exposing the way in which it works to
hide the structure of our desire, to conceal from us that we constitute reality by thinking it to ourselves, representing it to ourselves,
by "seeing" in it the same models of narrative coherence that we
have learned from such media as novels. To observe the proprieties
of realism, a novel must be perfectly fictitious, and yet perfectly
deferent to the real; a perfect reflection of reality, and yet inferior
to it, different in kind. Stendhal mocks this contradiction in his defense of Mathilde de La Mole as a narrative device: he is not to be
blamed for her "mimeticism," her controlled and calculated desire,
because she is completely fictitious, made up; on the other hand,

he is also innocent because, as a novelist, he merely transcribes reality without judging it. The ideology of realism wants to have its cake and eat it too. What does that make Mathilde? Real or imagined? It makes her, and the novel, *and the real itself*, both and neither.

The scandal, and the tragedy, here is that Julien and Mathilde may not know why or how they want what they want—any more than the shop girl pining over a picture of some shirtless rock star in a teen magazine, or the young upwardly mobile couple with a BMW, a money market fund, a subscription to *Gourmet* magazine, and a baby they are determined to send to Harvard, or the football fan who never misses a home game, or the collector of cars or stamps or coins or animals or sexual conquests, or the other minor characters of *The Red and the Black*, or for that matter critics who churn out boring articles and books about other books ad infinitum, without ever wondering why. The uniqueness, and the scandal, of this novel, is that it is determined to show us why we want what we want—why, in the first place, we want to read novels like this one.

7

The Guillotine; or, The Only Good Hero Is a Dead Hero

So Julien tries to murder Mme. de Rênal, on account of a letter which she in fact did not write, but copied, exactly as Julien had done with his letters to the widow Fervaques. Her priest wrote the letter for her, and she only "softened" some passages in copying it out. (We do not find out about this until very near the end of the novel.) Everyone here is copying someone or some text in everything they do; nothing is truly original except maladroitness, unwitting distortions of the "original" to be copied. Julien will lose his head over a murder that fails (Mme. de Rênal incurs only minor flesh wounds), inspired by a letter that the intended victim did not even compose. A comedy of errors, but a black one. Julien's failure to understand the circuit of desire in which he has been so absorbed will cost him his life.

But it will also consecrate him as the very sort of romantic hero he has wished to become. Mathilde de La Mole and Louise de Rênal, even the Abbé Chélan, even his jailors, are madly in love with Julien for what he has done. M. de Frilair thinks "it might be possible to make a martyr of him" (462). To Mathilde, his "crime" "reveals the loftiness of the heart beating in this breast" (464).

"You are still the superior man," she says, "he whom I have singled out!" (465). The parish priest sends him, in jail, bottles of excellent wine. His father, who used to despise him, comes to see him in jail, if only to ask for money (Julien even has some of that now—he is an object of desire in even the crassest terms, those which prevail in Verrières, that hypothetically prettiest and crassest of towns).

Julien is famous and admired, though no one really knows why. Something about his "crime"—not the crime of wishing to be an object of desire, but the more trivial one of having attempted to murder his former lover—has appealed, accidentally but also quite completely, to the popular imagination. After death, his remains are treated by his friend Fouqué and Mathilde de La Mole like those of a saint or a demigod, holy relics. Mathilde has the chance to repeat, almost perfectly, the part of Marguerite de Navarre in the story of Boniface de La Mole; she even considers suicide, for "what would the Paris drawing rooms say if they saw a lover condemned to die worshiped to that extent by a girl of my rank? To find like sentiments, you have to go back to the age of heroes; it was love affairs of this kind that set hearts to beating in the reign of Charles IX and of Henri III" (472).

One may well imagine Julien thinking, in the midst of such sentiments, "Well and good, I am glad you find the circumstances so thrilling, well and good for *you*, but I, Julien Sorel, am about to have my head violently removed, and, all romantic aspirations aside, I feel terrified and alone."

Nothing consecrates heroism like death. Julien, however, is not simply gratified to have gotten his wish. Heroes are not people for whom we have sympathy, but rather symbols we adapt to our own purposes. Julien, not yet merely a dead symbol, is frightened of death. He discovers a powerful nostalgia for the days of his affair with Mme. de Rênal, for the time when he was just beginning his progress toward superstardom and experiencing all sorts of things for the first time. With Mme. de Rênal there had been an immediacy born of their mutual awkwardness and inexperience, and a complicity in their plots to deceive her husband. With Mathilde, desire had been more a battle of wills, a contest of feint and counterfeit in which the awkwardness, though it remained, had no felicitous consequences and failed to charm either of the two protagonists. They had both long since become too jaded for that. At the end of his quest, Julien looks back to the beginning longingly, not to change anything, but with a nostalgia for the first time he tried to seduce someone, to enter the game of desire, and succeeded.

The horrible aspect of Julien's story is that there is no pleasure at all in dying, though death is really necessary to his apotheosis as the cultural icon he has always, unquestioningly, aspired to be. There is no fun in being a superstar, except in looking back to the past, to the way up. Perhaps most scandalous, there is no askesis for Julien, as there should be in any proper tragedy: Julien never seems to realize that this in fact is what he thought he wanted all along, or why or how he came to want it. This ending is, for the reader, hard to take.

But it has always, from the very first page, been inevitable. To become a superstar, a cultural icon, is to become a dehumanized symbol, an image on a billboard, a commodity, to lose one's individuality, to become obliterated by the desire of one's public. The ending of *The Red and the Black* must seem absolutely correct for anyone who has read the novel closely, and yet critics have continued to find the ending "scandalous," as though they had completely misread the first 450 pages, not recognizing any difference between this narrative and the standard Victorian novel with its inevitable happy ending: "The guillotine that so abruptly, perhaps unreasonably, puts an end to Julien Sorel's life and brilliant career has ever been a critical scandal, an outrage to coherent interpretation."[17]

I have tried to show in detail that Julien's desire is structured in such a way that he must be destroyed by his own success. The example of Napoleon is a vivid demonstration of this principle. In defeat and exile, Napoleon became far more powerful as a symbol than he could ever have been in victory. The vanquished hero attains mythic proportions in our imaginations that no mere mortal, despite heroic acts, can ever approach. If he had not lost, we would remember Napoleon as a tyrant, without any of the tragic proportions of a cultural icon. One cannot become a perfect object of desire except by being absent or, even better (because absolutely absent, unattainable, *lost*), dead. To quote Proust again, "the only true paradises are the ones that have been lost." What is true of places is also true of persons.

Many critics have said that the attempt on the life of Mme. de Rênal is insufficiently motivated. It also seems, in the light of my reading here, predictable, if implausible. Julien feels that his honor has been unfairly smeared, leaving him only one recourse: to avenge himself by destroying his betrayer, and to die for it—to die for his honor. To die himself would appear to be part of his calculations, since he chooses the most public of places, a church, to commit the murder. He could not possibly hope to escape. And though the option is held out to him, he refuses to appeal his death sentence. He fears death, but he seems to accept it as an almost aesthetic necessity. He seems to know what the novel tells us, that "never had that head [Julien's] been more poetical than at the moment it was about to fall" (507).

Of course, there is still something shockingly abrupt, unexpected, even implausible about Julien's decision to murder Mme. de Rênal. The act seems to flout such principles of realism as motivation and plausibility—as do other, lesser acts, such as Julien's earlier near murder of Mathilde de La Mole. But so does real life, much of the time. We do not expect our day-to-day experience to observe the proprieties of realistic representation; why then should we expect represented reality to observe them? *Vraisemblance* is to the novel as manners and wit are to the Parisian aristocracy. I alluded earlier to the fact that Stendhal has no interest in a strict observance of these conventions. A large part of the subject of his novel is the inadequacy and fallaciousness, the illusoriness and the downright foolishness, of just such conventions. I do not mean to suggest that Julien's attempted murder is sufficiently motivated, plausible according to the rules of realism, but rather that if we wish to make sense of Julien's act and subsequent demise in terms of the larger narrative, there are many ways of doing so, ways that are not inconsistent with Stendhal's narrative practices.

The way in which Julien dies has been suggested in many more cryptic ways in the novel.[18] The name of the town, Verrières, is a gloss on everything to come. A *verrière* in French is a window, containing the word *verre*, glass. Part of the ideology of realism is that the realistic text is supposed to be a window on reality, a perfectly transparent opening through which the real appears. Unironic (unsophisticated) literature always tries to make and sustain this claim. Verrières itself, as Stendhal describes it, with its absolute tyranny of public opinion, is a kind of text with extreme and unsophisticated claims to "realism." The people of the town are sure that their convictions (in which nothing is valuable unless it "brings in revenue") are the most correct, the most practical and "realistic" one could possibly have. The notion that others might see the world differently in a different place would appear to them completely, scandalously wrongheaded—and disturbing, a transgression against "common sense."

The town (a glass window or windows—there is an *s* on it) also constitutes an optic in which Julien is, in the beginning, undesirable, worthless. He has to shatter that lens, as Stendhal's narrative voice aims to shatter the invisibility of mimetic desire and mimetic realism, expose their pretenses to transparency as a sham, in the construction of his story. Both Julien and his author have sought to break the conventions that, like a trick glass or mirror, pretend to show us what is "real" while concealing how desire works to create the illusion. To go through, past the window (*verrière*) of realism, Julien must "break" the illusion of which he is part, violate the limitations of his time and place. He has not sought to attain any distance of understanding from that realistic optic or ideology, however; he has no sense of irony—no distance of understanding—about himself or his ambitions with which to shield himself from all the broken glass. Julien has identified completely with the very milieus (Verrières, the Rênal household, the aristocracy of Paris), the very mimetic desire that he has sought to transgress. By breaking the rules of mimetic desire (according to which the desire of Julien, to be a model of the desire of others, is illicit and transgressive) Julien breaks himself.

Nicholas Rand has pointed out that the word for the aperture of the guillotine in which the condemned's neck is placed, *lunette*, also designates "a semicircular window in a vaulted roof." Julien breaks through the window only to find his neck caught in the hole, and a blade suspended above: instead of going entirely through the window, as the narrator of the novel does, in order to look back on it, Julien tries to transgress while remaining within, to exceed, to supersede convention while remaining within it. This leaves his head outside the edifice of convention and his body inside, his neck situated in a place where convention (closure, the necessity of a formal end to the story) is bound to cut it. The guillotine would thus represent the central, governing metaphor of mimetic realism (the transparent window or lens), and Julien gets caught in this metaphor, halfway in and halfway out, so that when closure comes, as it is bound (formally) to do, it must split him into two pieces, one on the side of naive mimeticism, and one on the side of an ironic skepticism with regard to mimetic conventions.

The realistic text—and Julien makes himself into a figure of such texts by seeking to shape his life according to models of realistic narrative—cannot survive the breakage of the conventions on which it is built except through irony, by keeping a certain distance from its own realistic pretensions and even mocking them. The narrative voice of *The Red and the Black* exemplifies such an irony, which ends the novel by telling us: "The bad thing about the reign of public opinion, which, it must be added, procures *liberty*, is that it meddles with that which is none of its business: for instance, private life. Hence, America's and England's gloominess. To avoid infringing upon any private life, the author has invented a small town, Verrières, and when he needed a bishop, a jury, an assize court, he situated them all in Besançon, where he has never been" (508–9).

The only possible refuge from the "tyranny" of public opinion (that is, of mimetic desire) is in the folds and crannies of an ironic (self-aware) fiction such as this one, which always refuses to state its relation to the real—or to itself—simply. Julien has never embraced such an irony with respect to himself, to the text(s) of which he is part and emblem: those of Verrières, of the seminary, of Paris, of the novel called *The Red and the Black*. He has never been aware of the ironies in his own successes. He has taken the conventions of mimeticism as seriously as the most unsophisticated realistic novel, or the most unsophisticated reader, and made himself absolutely one with those conventions. His every act has been dictated by the principle of mimeticism, of imitation, yet his success depends on exceeding, superseding those conventions. To supersede, while remaining within, is both transgression and apotheosis. Julien's head is severed by the glass(es) he has finally broken through. It never occurred to him that a piece of this glass might fall on him, but when it does, he accepts it as a reasonable end to his story.

By cutting off the head of his main character, Stendhal "truncates" his narrative in unseemly fashion: so critics speaking for the conventions of realism have charged. But Stendhal has already made it clear that his purpose is not to celebrate mimeticism but to expose it, to cut it open and show us how it works. The first "cut" in the text does not occur at the end, any more than Julien's first death wish. Stendhal's "realistic novel" is marked on nearly every page by the incisions of the narrator's commentaries on it, his theoretical intrusions to point out that causality and motivation, all the unspoken premises of mimetic realism (in both the Aristotelian and the Girardian sense), are arbitrary and illusory. The novel, as an instance of mimeticism, is bleeding from a myriad of small cuts, exposing its insides to the reader's view, long before Julien (and the narrative) feel the cold steel of closure.

If there is a moral here it must be this: we cannot escape mimetic desire—mass culture—by mere transgression of it, for in transgression, there is affirmation and acceptance; this is as true for the football fanatic as for the teenager smitten by some poster of a movie star, for the college professor of literature as for the reader of *Playboy*. There is no possibility of escape, but there may be some solace in a (stoic) understanding of the ways in which our desire is always copying and being copied. Such an understanding cannot forget that it is also subject to the very mimeticism, the very ironies, that it sees, and that it cannot see in itself. (Blindness to the possibility of its own misunderstanding, to its own ironies, is the premise of every act of understanding; there are examples of this on every page of *The Red and the Black*.) Another solace, or happiness, might be possible, in which the subject embeds itself so completely in the patterns of mimetic desire that it forgets them, and they remain invisible. This is a dumb happiness, entirely ignorant of its own workings, and also fragile, because it depends so much on the desires of others. The ironic stance of Stendhal's narrator does not constitute a real escape from mimetic desire, but starts from the premise that no real escape is possible: our desire is then not only vulnerable to manipulation, but is *defined* by manipulation—willing, conscious, or not.

Shoshana Felman has argued that all this means that Julien is "mad" (*fou*). The "madman," according to her, "is one who has no language in common with his peers, and whose solitary word fails to make itself understood."[19] Even as astute a critic as Ann Jefferson has been willing to agree with Felman.[20] I would say that, according to this definition, they are completely wrong. Julien is nothing if not a master of languages—of Latin, eventually of

French, and of all the social languages of etiquette and wit—in short, he is a quick learner of all the languages of desire, and he succeeds in using them, and in being used by them, to make the kind of story, the kind of spectacle, he wants to make, the spectacle of superstardom.

Does Julien turn out to have been crazy in some other way? Felman says that madness is an essential ingredient of all of Stendhal's heroes, and of many of his minor characters. This need not make her reading incompatible with mine:

> The act of madness (*l'acte fou*) is, in essence, a forgetfulness that remembers itself: a spontaneous, radical act that erases one level of being to accede to another—an act of rupture that reconnects with something lost. The forgetfulness signifies, thus, a recall, the existential upheaval of some original forgotten thing: the rupture with a present state recuperates, at the same time, something archaic, primordial. (Felman, 52)

> Stendhalian "madness": an interior discrepancy felt by the characters of the novel with respect to their *hic et nunc* [here and now], to their immediate circumstances. (Felman, 54)

> All the characters, in fact, live in the grip of fancy. They are incapable of a neutral look: the way in which they see things always bears the imprint of an ideal and imaginary model. (Felman, 62)

If madness is an "interior discrepancy" in which subjects look to and identify with models of desire from another place or time, from books, and in which their relation to the real is conditioned and even determined by their imaginary identification with such models of desire, then this madness must be an extremely common symptom of the sort of desire, and the sort of culture, that I have been talking about, and Stendhal has been representing (and mocking) in *The Red and the Black*. Such madness would be not an exception but a rule. We must, indeed, all be very much in the grip of this madness. It is the very foundation of our mass culture.

While wrong in her definition of it, Felman is right to call this phenomenon madness, if only to point out how dangerous it may be unless we are fully cognizant of it. To be aware of it may not make us any less mad. It may, however, give us a certain degree of distance from our madness. Then again, it may not.

What sense does this reading make of the novel's title? What did Stendhal mean by "red" and "black"? It has always been thought that he chose these colors for his title because they signify several different things. Red was the color of the uniforms of the French Revolutionary and Napoleonic army, and black the color worn by priests. These two colors thus stand for the two careers in which a young man like Julien might hope to advance. Bishops, though, also wear red, and the movement from black to red would also signify advancement within the ranks of the clergy. Red and black are, moreover, the colors of the roulette wheel, pointing to the recurrent motif of accident, of luck, in Julien's story. Red is also the color of blood, and black that of mourning and death, the colors of Julien's death as of his life.

There is also in the title an allusion to the text's own "scandalousness." Texts are not red and black, but white and black. This one, however, is "stained," on every page, by the small "incisions" made in it by its narrator's ironic intrusions, and by the very large incision made in Julien's neck at the end. Julien's blood, as it were, has stained realism's claims to purity, stained the white pages red. The place where Julien's final "cut" (decapitation) occurs is the location of the realistic text itself, suspended in the tension of its contradictions, between life, which imitates art (but isn't supposed to), and art, which is supposed to be imitating life. The violence, the bleeding seam—*redness*—of that contradiction between what realism says it is doing (imitating "life") and what it is in fact also doing (giving "life" models to imitate) is the subject of *The Red and the Black*. The black print of the book is about, and situated upon, the red: the bloody, violent contradictions of mimetic realism.

Did Stendhal have all these considerations in mind when choosing his title? Probably not. By saying so, I admit that literary criticism and scholarship are subject to the same sort of internal contradictions ("bloodiness") as realism. (It doesn't make any sense to talk about what a title is supposed to mean unless we assume that the author meant something by it.) In a book on Stendhal, it seems particularly important to acknowledge these contradictions explicitly. By admitting them, by thus taking an ironic stance toward the critical enterprise, we do not escape them, any more in a text of this sort than in *The Red and the Black*.

Finally, it is worth asking how this novel seems different from those of the two other great French realists of the nineteenth century, Flaubert and Balzac. Stendhal's practice differs markedly from both in that he spends very little time on the description of physical settings. His longest descriptions are of characters' thoughts, rather than their clothes or rooms. Flaubert's understanding of the way desire works in modern culture is really the same as Stendhal's, but the way in which he represents it is quite different. Flaubert's irony is carefully embedded *in* his fictions, not directly visible. His narrative voice never comments directly on his characters. Flaubert seeks rather to transcribe mimetic desire, using all the resources of mimetic representation, than to point to it directly. Stendhal talks openly about how mimetic desire and fictional realism work. Flaubert shows it working in and on his characters and his readers by carefully deploying all the "special effects" of literary realism to cause us to suspend disbelief, to know that we are doing so, and yet to read as though we did not know, to take pleasure simultaneously in the fact of artifice and the success of it. We take a similar pleasure in a film that uses lots of special effects: we know they are not "real," and yet we take pleasure in them both as sophisticated artifice (special effects) and as though we did believe in their reality (suspending disbelief). Stendhal's narratives might be called hybrid: mostly fiction, but with liberal doses of essay, literary criticism, and cultural/literary theory added here and there. Stendhal's narrator is quite visible, or audible, at all times, while Flaubert's remains—seeks to remain—always out of sight, hidden like a puppeteer by curtains and black clothing.

Neither Stendhal nor Flaubert believed, as Balzac wished to believe, that there are objective "structures" and "types" in human society that may be cataloged in fiction, as science in the eighteenth century had undertaken to catalog the forms of life on earth, on the model of the encyclopedia. The science of happiness, of human desire, is for Stendhal, and for Flaubert, different in kind from every other science. We might with reason call Balzac the most positivist of the three, with his belief in fiction as a mode of scientific, taxonomic research in the structures of human society. We might call Flaubert the most pure in his deployment of the resources of mimetic, realistic fiction to seduce the literary desire of sophisticated readers—appealing to their pleasure in artifice—while depicting that same mimetic desire in his characters. We might say that Stendhal was the most playfully innovative with the conventions of the realistic novel, combining it with other nonfiction genres to achieve a kind of hybrid text that explicitly puts into question its own premises, that exposes, comments on, and mocks the very conventions it must depend on—that quite openly deconstructs itself.

8

Literature and History

In this chapter I consider some more abstract aspects of the relation between literature and history that are implied by *The Red and the Black*. This is, more than most written in the nineteenth century, a novel *about* the relation of literature to history, imagination to memory. It is known that the novel was inspired by two newspaper accounts, one of a cabinetmaker named Lafargue who decapitated his mistress, and another about a seminarian named Antoine Berthet who tried to kill his benefactress in a church because (apparently) she would not sleep with him. The story of Berthet, a frail young man of humble origins who was adopted by a curate and taken on as tutor by a wealthy family, is very close to that of Julien Sorel. In a similar way, Flaubert was inspired to write *Madame Bovary*. If these newspaper accounts are a part of what we call "history," then history is not so much different in kind from literature, but rather a different sort of text, subject to different requirements in its relation to actual events. In the phenomenon we call realism, which is still very much the dominant mode of literary expression in our culture, literature takes as object and incitement not "life" directly (which may not even be possible) but verbal accounts of it: journalism, history.

The nineteenth was of course the century most preoccupied with history and literary history: the century of the most historically, positivistically oriented of critics (Hippolyte Taine, Charles Sainte-Beuve) and the most literary of historians (Jules Michelet, the Goncourt brothers). History became the province of literature and vice versa. Julien Sorel has come to represent, in the historical consciousness of France, an entire generation that came of age at the time of the Restoration, before the Revolution of 1830, and he is neither a historical personage nor a historical fiction, but some strange tension between the two.

What defines Julien, more than anything else, are (1) ambition, which amounts to a talent for *imagining* the political and social possibilities of the (his) future, and (2) a keen sense of history—of *memory* (remember his remarkable gift for languages and for memorization). The novel is in one sense about the relation between these two faces of human consciousness, imagination and memory, which quickly become figures for the dialectical opposition of literature and history. Julien is "created," defined by the tension between these two poles, both thematically (within the novel) and as a text, because of the way in which *The Red and the Black* was inspired and written.

In a passage already cited in chapter 6, Stendhal's narrator commits a brazen contradiction to justify his literary project, and as he does so, he gives some idea of the deep, irreducible contradiction embodied in the idea of "historical fiction" or, even, of literary history. The character of Mathilde de La Mole is supposed to be "altogether imaginary and, in fact, imagined well outside the pale of . . . social customs" (358). Yet he goes on to describe the novel as a mirror that does not invent but merely reflects. Some critics might see only facetiousness here. I believe there is more. Later in the novel there occurs another intrusion by the narrator in which we are told that he would have preferred to present the reader with "a page of dots" rather than to reproduce the political (historical) debate to which Julien was witness. This is not permissible, however, for the sake of "taste": the book's hypothetical "editor" interjects that "in a piece of writing as frivolous as this, bad taste is death" (378). The political, and by implication the historical, the "author" replies, is "a millstone around the neck of literature and will sink it in less than six months. Politics in the midst of imaginary concerns is like a pistol shot in the middle of a concert. The noise is ear-splitting without being energetic. It does not harmonize with any instrument" (378). But without it, without history, "the editor rejoined, 'they are not Frenchmen of 1830, and your book is not the mirror you claim it to be' " (378). Indeed, the book is no longer anything but a sequence of ellipses.

Of course, the debate that is "reproduced" is not historical in the sense of having occurred, not remembered, but imagined. Its coincidence with the real historical events of 1830 was, however, highly provocative at the time. The novel's writing must then be motivated by an ambition not unlike Julien's own: the desire to transform itself from its origins, as imagination, into history, the narrative of reality. Julien, remember, means to repeat, to "become," the story of Napoleon (or someone like Napoleon), to realize (to "remember" backward, to project) the future he has imagined for himself by remembering the past. Yet the passage cited above says clearly that, though the novel (imagination) cannot do without history (memory), yet history will submerge it. The issue would appear to be not *whether* the novel is submerged, but *when*—either now, because of bad taste, or at some indeterminate time in the future. Pursuing history for the moment affords only a temporary pardon, a "grace period" (Stendhal uses the French word *grâce* for "taste"), which must still in the end become a *coup de grâce*. The French word *grâce* applies to both clemency and execution. It is in that clemency, that reluctant, wary, and doomed embrace of history, that the novel must enact its desire, its life, seeking to define itself in terms of history and yet to remain somehow apart from it.

This also perfectly describes Julien's situation. His execution is the end of the novel. Julien's death, his decapitation (the actual narration of which is omitted from the book) is the moment in which there is no longer any difference between literature (imagination) and history, and Julien's imagined (through memory) future, as an object of worship, is realized. We might say that "superstardom" occurs where the difference between the imaginary and the real, the historical, breaks down. But neither our sense of reality nor our sense of the literary can survive that breakdown, except as lifeless, inert "pieces" of a former life.

The moment in which the difference between the literary (imaginary) and the historical breaks down is also the moment in which the figure of their difference and their mutual involvement, Julien, is "split" into two fragments that, no longer animated, remain very much "alive"—more so than ever, in fact—as an object and a paradigm of desire, a narrative, a story, for others. By signifying a "reality" (an individual, a life, a story) that is now absent from them, Julien's remains exert a powerful attraction on those around him. Both the literary and the historical would seem to depend for their "lives" on being connected, on mutual contamination; yet each strains toward a kind of discreteness, independence, which once achieved, extinguishes both. And yet they survive, more powerful than ever, because they now stand for a narrative of loss (like Napoleon), in the remnants of their former mutual involvement, as the "idol" of superstardom, in the adoring eyes and desires of Mme. de Rênal, Fouqué, Mathilde de La Mole—and us, witnesses also of Julien's demise and apotheosis. We know imagination and memory most intensely through the mediation of death, as a story of loss; we know literature and history through the narrative, which tells of their mutual involvement and estrangement, and which ends by breaking the figure that stood for both into fragments that become fetishes, idols, which we value because they signify something absent from them. Isn't this the definition of a text? A collection of fragments (words, letters) that refer to something outside, beyond themselves, something lost (the real, or "history")?

At this point the concept of "inverted imagination" takes on a new importance: "in this state of *inverted imagination*, he [Julien] undertook to judge life with his imagination. This is the error of a superior man" (360). Julien can apprehend the world, or himself in the world, only by imagining how it and he look in the imaginations of others. He imagines himself, then he imagines how others imagine themselves, then he imagines how others imagine him. This describes rather well how literature and history "see" one another. The "real" is an illusion produced by the dialectic of imagination between literature and history, each conceiving itself in a relation of difference from the other: imagining itself, the one imagining the other, then imagining a difference inscribed within the other. The real would be something implied by this imaginary difference of literature from history and history from literature, the difference imagined by each within the other, constituting each by its difference from the other, in the eyes of the other. This is the same way that Julien imagines himself (in a relation of difference from others who imagine him), and the way in which human perception creates the real as a category apart from perception, by inference, as a residue of this inverted imagining. The real, as something independent of imagination, is an "error," but the error, Stendhal says, of "a superior man." The sentence does not imply that only superior men make errors, but that inferior men make lesser mistakes. What might the error of an inferior man be? Perhaps to take the real not as a residue of imagination, not as a novelist composing a novel, but as a historian or journalist, imparting to it an existence independent of imagination.

It is inverted imagination that prevents Julien from ending the novel prematurely:

> The idea of suicide occurred to him several times; it seemed a charming notion; he thought of it as a delightful rest; it was the glass of ice water held out to the wretch in the desert who is dying of thirst and heat.
>
> "My death will make her even more contemptuous of me!" he cried. "What a memory I shall leave!" (360)

Death would be the point at which the novel, Julien, literature and history, are split, and Julien's *cou de grâce* (his neck, which holds the two parts of him, imagination and memory, literature and history, head and body, together in a temporary clemency of life) becomes a *coup de grâce*, a blow, a gesture, a space, a void, which ends Julien's life and makes it into a story. Yet his *cou* has always been synonymous with the *coup* that severs it: "Julien is no more; it is his corpse that moves" (364).

What is imagination in the novel but *memory reversed*, a projection, based on expectation or fear or wish, of bits and pieces—severed fragments—of the past into some hypothetical totality, some would-be present or past? Our experience of the present, our decoding of the messages given us in the present, is made possible by the dictionary of memory, our mental registry of the past. Julien is defined by and his advancement is conditioned on memory, and specifically on a memory of words, the capacity to recite, his knowledge of languages and his reading. "Julien is no more; it is his corpse that moves"—in French, the verb *vivre*, to live, in the first part of the sentence appears as *vit* ("Julien ne vit plus"), which could be present or literary past tense (*passé simple*), though the second verb, *s'agiter*, to move, is unambiguously in the present. What is Julien's "corpse" if not the corpus of words that narrate him, that we imagine as though they were remembered being spoken by him? The clemency (*grâce*) in which the novel, and Julien's life, transpires is as much an illusion as reality, a phenomenon of imagination. The time after which literature must be submerged by history is already long over. The novel is already indistinct from what we understand to be historical, dissolved in it, lost in it, and never existed apart from it except through the illusion of inverted imagination.

The images that make up what we think of as reality are inseparable from *ima*gination. Imagination contains those images we think of as real, and repeats them. Both words are from the Latin *imago* (likeness or copy). The Latin verb *imaginari* is to make images, copies, likenesses. Imagination is not contrary to reality but a likeness of it. We cannot understand reality—come up with a working model, a likeness of it—without the help of imagination. The only difference between imaginary images and real images is direction, whether we are projecting outward or inward. Inverted imagination and inverted image are the same thing. Inverted imagination is the name Stendhal uses for Julien's way of perceiving himself in the world, by imagining the way others see him; inverted image would describe the way in which the novel proceeds, as a "mirror" of reality that also sees itself as part of reality, that can only imagine itself in and through the eyes of the real, in a relation of difference and resemblance with the real, or history.

A mirror reflects the persons looking into it, author and reader. Certainly, there is nothing in the nature of the optic to make those reflected images identical, only properties that will subject them to the same degree of distortion. Literature does not simply reflect history but produces it, like a copy machine in reverse, one that produces originals from copies. It is the mirror that makes possible the illusion of the "highway's" reality. How else to explain how, as in the passage cited earlier, the novel as "mirror" might reflect what does not and "could not" exist (Mathilde de la Mole)? How could a copy be made from an original that does not exist, unless we are in the business of making originals from copies? How can the mind recall what never happened? Of course this is just what the novel (fiction) does, and also what Julien does within the novel. Julien, as a literary "corpse," remembers what did not really happen, mixed up with what did (the life of Napoleon). A real mirror can show only what is, the moment. Julien and the novel are verbal, figural mirrors, not real ones, and they are able to reflect what an actual glass cannot: memory, or memory inverted, imagination. Fiction is like a mirror because it shows an image that is like us and yet different from us, that is only a corpse/corpus and yet "moves" in the duration of a "clemency" that has already expired.

The corpse/corpus is made to move by the tension of an illusory distinction (inverted imagination) between literature and history. It is this dialectic, of likeness and difference, that causes us to lend life to the corpse, to suspend disbelief, to lend credence to the independent being of Julien, the "highway" of the novel. We "see" (imagine) an image, and yet the optic of words, unlike that of glass, distorts it in such a way that we sustain belief that it is not our own image we see but that of another, of an author, of a voice within the mirror. The corpse "sits up and talks" to us. And of course we are the only ones moving or speaking. The only reason we are supposed to bother with literature, with fiction, is that it provides access to the real, to history as the great ongoing, endless highway of the real, the lost original from which all copies are made. But in fact, the original is inferred from the copies.

The real is the original (in the sense of "having to with origin") in which we all believe ourselves, our personal stretches of highway, to figure. It is the great lens in which everyone and everything is supposed to be reflected at once, all time and space. It is what we come from and where we end. It is because of this sense of the real, of a great "original" to which we all belong, that literature and history draw and hold our attention. Literature and history, together, make a sort of metaphysical copy machine that spews out copies from that original, thereby sustaining belief in the latter. It is that illusion of an absent, original, and final totality (reality) realized by *inverted imagination*, the illusion of a reality distinct from our perception and yet including it, which prevents Julien's suicide, and that of literature (or history). It is the ambition to have a decent memory, to be inscribed honorably in the great fiction of totality (history) that keeps Julien from ending his story too soon, and his death is his inscription in that "real." His life (his story) occurs as a static noise caused by the mutual interference of literature and history, and is punctuated at both ends by silence. The novel is a dissonance in history as history is a dissonance in the novel: each, within the other, is like a pistol shot at a concert.

History claims to be "nearer" the real than literature. It might be thought of as the first step in rendering the real literary by inverted imagination; history represents the process by which the real is inferred by the use of imagination. We do not think of ourselves as inferring it, but rather assume its independent existence. Literature would be the second stage of inverted imagination, in which history is fed back through the process of inverted imagination (we imagine the real, then we imagine it looking back at us) and emerges as "fiction," which is involved with the historical in a relation of resemblance. Literature is a sort of ghost of the real; or we might say that the real is a sort of ghost, an absence that is constantly referred to, that haunts both literature and history, animating the corpse/corpus of texts and making them appear to move. Both fiction and history are haunted this way; both look to whatever is beyond them, outside the circuit of inverted imagination, to give them life. We might say they look to death to give themselves life.

Death is not a thing that can be represented. Everything that leads up to Julien's decapitation is narrated, but not his actual death. Death, like reality—as part of reality—can only be inferred through inverted imagination. In the dance between literature and history, imagination and memory, haunted by the real and by death, the corpse/corpus of Julien Sorel moves, the dead live, and what cannot be represented or thought is given a name, even if it may be an arbitrary, imaginary one.

We have seen how, in Stendhal's novelistic paradigm, desire and ambition follow the model of reading, which functions by inverted imagination too. All of his characters seek to repeat some cultural or historical model of desire in their own behavior, whether love or work, about which they have heard or read, in newspapers, historical accounts, or novels. The act of living as Stendhal represents it is thus a repeated reversal of the act of imagining, a "naming" of the self (which is essentially unrepresentable, like death) after various examples. This act of naming, of imitating, has always to be repeated because it cannot be finished, achieved, short of being subsumed by death.

This repetition and imitation blurs distinctions of time, space, and identity. "The Russians copy French ways, but always fifty years behind the times" (393). M. de Rênal is "prompt to copy the ways of court society" (57). Mathilde finds the young men around her all "pale copies of one another" (357). "All France copies Paris" (386). All likenesses of some misplaced original (again in the sense of primal, of origin)? And yet, those things to which the word *original* is applied by critics are representations, likenesses. The real origin is always elsewhere.

Something is called original when it enacts a repetition that seems to efface the thing repeated, and to overwhelm the very act of repeating, naming. Originality, then, is a representation, a repetition, that works some sort of violence on what it repeats, that turns away from its origin in the same way that Julien turns away from his. And yet originality must finally be another illusion created by inverted imagination, however violently it turns away from the origin it looks to. Representation dare not turn too far away from its object, or it becomes no longer original but random, no longer a harmony but a pistol shot. Repetition, to qualify as original, must enact both difference and resemblance. Thus proper comportment in society is always a matter of learning one's lines and repeating them flawlessly, but also of making it appear that the lines are completely spontaneous. This is where Julien excels. As Prince Korasoff says to him, "I will be frank to say that your role is a difficult one; you will be playing a part in a comedy, but if anyone guesses that you are acting, you are done for" (394). This same paradox of natural artifice, artificial nature, is of course François de La Rochefoucauld's *honnêteté* ("honesty") and the subject of Denis Diderot's treatise *Paradoxe sur le comédien* (Paradox of the actor).

It is the very same paradox that is represented by inverted imagination and that the historical novel seeks to enact, as a mirror reflecting (repeating, naming) something that is not, that it can approach only through the mediation of another mirror (history), the newspaper, and that is, however, by definition beyond mediation, unnameable: the "imaginarily" real. The experience of all the characters in *The Red and the Black* is a constant reversal of repetition: repeat, say your lines perfectly, but turn them, invert them, and so achieve originality in the eyes of the world and of your own inverted imagination: "*always do the contrary of what is expected of you*" (281). Name yourself, repeat the "names" and desires of others and copy them onto your own, but inverted, and then—this is the work of originality—carve the characters of these names and desires, now yours, onto the faces and desires of others.

> "But, to be sure, gentlemen, you will carry my mark; I will aim for your faces, like Caesar's soldiers at Pharsala. . . . As for the letters, I can put them in a safe place."
> Julien made copies of the last two, hid them in a volume of the library's handsome Voltaire, and took the originals to the post himself. (336)

The connection here between the literal copying of letters and the figure of making one's "marks" on the face (*figure*, in French, means both face and figure, in the sense of shape or rhetoric, figure of speech) of others is no less striking for being one of contingency rather than outright analogy. The analogy is clearly implied. This act of repetition and naming is directly and repeatedly allied in the novel with the act of reading; remember how Julien got his distaste for eating with the servants from Rousseau.

Desire is enacted on the same model. Mathilde is drawn to Julien because he does not seem like a copy, but an original, and because, by pure happenstance, a "contingent" act, she copies him, repeats his likeness.

> While she made these reflections Mathilde, so as not to betray her thoughts to her mother's watchful eye, kept sketching haphazardly on a

page of her album. One of the profiles she had just finished amazed, delighted her: it bore a striking resemblance to Julien. "This is the voice of heaven! Here is one of love's miracles," she said to herself ecstatically. "Unwittingly I have drawn his portrait."

> She flew to her room, locked herself in, found some colors, applied herself and tried in earnest to draw Julien's portrait, but she could not bring it off. The profile set down by chance was still the best likeness. Mathilde was delighted with it; in it she saw proof positive of a great passion. (357)

Stendhal's choice of words here, his saying that she *could* not succeed in drawing Julien rather than that she *did* not, suggests that there may be more of accident than of will in what we call successful originality in realistic art—originality, that is, in representing, copying real things and people.

Julien's seduction of Madame de Rênal is an enactment of what he has read, helped along by the "names" that others have given him.

> Perhaps Julien was a bit heartened by the remark "good-looking boy" which he had been hearing the girls repeat every Sunday for the past six months. (39)

> Some of the things Napoleon says about women, several discussions about the merits of novels that were fashionable during his reign, gave Julien, for the first time in his life, a few of the notions any other young man of his age would have come by long before then. (59)

> When Julien left Mme. de Rênal's bedroom some hours later, it might be said, in the style of the novel, that he had nothing more to desire. He was, in fact, obliged to the love he had inspired, and to the unexpected impression her seductive charms had made on him, for a conquest that all his clumsy maneuvering could never have brought off. (95)

Again in the last passage, the success of desire—*mimetic* desire in the sense of a desire that imitates other desires, the desires of others—is attributed more to accident than to will. Mme. de Rênal is in fact seduced by Julien's innocence and ignorance of women, and yet Julien, in order to seduce her at all, to even make the attempt, must play for himself the part of womanizer.

> "Have I failed in any way with respect to what I owe myself? Have I played my part well?"
> Which part? That of a man who is used to having his way with women. (96)

Julien has failed in his intended role—at least to everyone but himself—but succeeded brilliantly in another one. His success in the second was made possible by his failure in the first. Mme. de Rênal "names" Julien, "reads" him entirely differently from the way in which he seeks to name himself or have himself be read, or understood. Yet her misunderstanding or understanding (what we call it depends on our perspective) of his role is what allows it to succeed, what allows Julien to succeed in seducing her. For the imitation (of a man who is used to having his way with women) to succeed, it must fail. And though it succeeds, it cannot enjoy its success for its failure: "In a word, what made Julien a superior person was precisely what kept him from relishing the happiness that lay at his feet. He was like the sixteen-year-old girl with a lovely complexion who, when she goes to a ball, has the crazy notion of putting rouge on her face" (95).

This means that desire proceeds in much the same fashion as historical fiction, as realistic literature. It cannot succeed except by depending on something outside of it (history, "reality"). If representation, literature, art, succeed, it is because they succeed as art, not because they ever succeed in transcribing anything real. Still, realistic art and literature cannot enjoy their own success for asking the same questions as Julien: "Have I played my role well? Have I failed in any of my duties to myself?"

In a similar way, Mathilde de La Mole seeks to reenact history in her relations with Julien. Julien "succeeds" in this role, which he is quite unaware of playing, by threatening to kill her. "Mlle. de La Mole watched him in astonishment. 'Well, I've just missed being

killed by my lover!' she told herself. This idea carried her back to
the finest years in the reign of Charles IX and Henry III" (348). The
success of this role depends upon death, the threat of it, Julien's
more than Mathilde's:

> "Alas!" Mathilde said to herself, "at the court of Henry III one found
> men who were as great by character as by birth! Ah! If only Julien had
> served at Jarnac or at Moncontour, I should have no doubts. . . . A
> man's life was a game of chance. Civilization and the prefect of police
> have driven away chance; the unexpected has been banished. Should it
> appear in ideas, it is epigrammed to death; if it shows up in events, no
> measure is too cowardly for our fear. No matter what piece of madness
> fear may lead us to commit, it is excused. Degenerate and boring age!
> What would Boniface de La Mole have said if, raising his severed head
> from the grave in 1793, he had seen seventeen of his descendants let
> themselves be taken like sheep, to be guillotined two days later? Death
> was certain, yet it would have been bad form to defend oneself and kill
> a Jacobin or two. Ah! in the heroic age of France, in Boniface de La
> Mole's day, Julien would have been the major, and my brother the
> young priest with the right ideas, with caution in his eyes and reason on
> his tongue." (329–30)

Of course, it is as the headless Boniface that Julien has already
been cast in Mathilde's private reenactment of her family's history.
This threat and certainty of death, and of a chance that imposes it
without regard for logic, choice, or causality, is the most essential
aspect of history. The real allure of historical narrative is not story
so much as ending, death, the idea of time as finite. The idea of
time as finished, closed, is one that history cannot describe or
name, cannot narrate—it can only tell the stories of individual endings, small instances of apparent closure—but from which it
nevertheless perpetually derives its authority.

Desire depends on a similar paradox. To succeed, to be
requited, desire must be reciprocated by another, symmetrical desire. And this second desire necessarily contests the authority of
the first, the first's "origin-ality," even as, responding to the first,
the second desire allows the first one to succeed. The situation is

like that of two readers contesting the interpretation of a text. Their readings, by contesting one another, affirm the primacy of the text (as object of interpretation, interpretive desire), and yet only by identifying with it. Each seeks to monopolize the originality of the text. The text's originality is affirmed by each reader as each contests the other's interpretive claim. The only sure stabilization of the text, final affirmation of its primacy over any and all readers, would be the death of reading—and of the text, inasmuch as texts must be read in order to be texts. Any object of readerly desire is another desire, which copies it and which it copies; and yet its satisfaction depends on an illusion of independence, originality.

It might be objected that a reader confronts not a desire but an inanimate object in the text. But the text, insofar as it is read, is not an object at all but a reading. It is an inscription of the desire of its writer and perhaps also of those critics whose "re-writings" (readings) have become part of the canonically accepted understanding of the text. Every reader reads a reading, or many readings, just as everyone who desires desires another desire, or often several others at once. The tension created by this paradoxical repetition is what makes the corpse of any book "move."

Julien, as a figure for this text, is made to move and speak by the tension of many desires within the text, but principally those of Mme. de Rênal and Mathilde de La Mole. When these come into direct conflict, however, and one threatens the other's success, as when Mme. de Rênal sends her letter to Mathilde's father, impugning Julien's motives in marrying Mathilde, the outcome is Julien's attempt on her life and, ultimately, his own execution. There is a contest ("staged," as it were, by Stendhal) to control the direction of Julien's story, and the outcome of that contest is his death and the end of that story.

But Julien's end does not put an end to the desires of the two women for him. He has always, already, in the long run, been dead. Julien, immobilized, has become the analogue of a "definitive edition," an idol before which Mathilde (as reader/desirer) kneels as she never did while he yet "moved":

> She lit several candles. By the time Fouqué had the strength to look at her, she had set Julien's head on a little marble table and was kissing it on the brow. . . .
>
> Having stayed behind with Fouqué, she insisted on burying her lover's head with her own hands. Fouqué nearly went mad with grief over this.
>
> Through Mathilde's good offices, the rough cave was ornamented at great expense with marbles carved in Italy. (508)

The strange thing about texts, and objects of desire, as Stendhal's great admirer Proust knew so well, is that even after death they survive, animated by the desire that had named, repeated, *created* them in the first place. The desire moves long after the demise of its object.

The title of the novel may as well be understood in light of this phenomenon. Colors defy any definitive interpretation, though virtually every reader of Stendhal has speculated about the possible meanings of "red" and "black." The two words must finally be names given to visual, chromatic phenomena. Black is made up of all other colors, a summation of every other color, of too much color to the point of no color. All colors of the spectrum, together, absorb all light and reflect none, and thus have no color but darkness. Red is contained within black, and refers to black as part to whole. So it refers to what contains but exceeds or transcends it as color. So desire (Eros) in its pursuit of individual objects names and repeats small, individual versions of its real object: absolute possession, immobilization of the object and itself, death (Thanatos). Every reader enacts similar repetitions. So the realistic novel repeats history and becomes part of it. History, in turn, seeks to repeat everything, all human knowledge and experience, and becomes part of them. Historical fiction enacts, on a small scale, the endings that lend history its authority. And it looks to history to confirm its own authority. Novel and history face each other like two mirrors, reversing and repeating ad infinitum. This relation makes real closure, any final understanding, impossible, and yet sustains the illusion of their possibility. It is finally meaning—if meaning depends on closure—that is dead for the novel and for history. And yet, like Julien, *le cadavre s'agite*; whenever we look at the "corpse," read it, it still sits up and recites its lines, struts its role on the stage of our imagination. So too the realistic novel and history. Our object is to understand the darkness that is beyond understanding. The nearest we can come to it are names, stories: light, color. There is only black to see, but we can see only red.[21]

Notes and
References

1. Cited in Claude Roy, *Stendhal* (Paris: Seuil, 1951), 169. My translation.

2. *Promenades dans Rome*, ed. Henri Martineau (Paris, 1931), 2:182–83.

3. See Jean Starobinski's "Stendhal pseudonyme," in *L'Oeil vivant* (Paris: Gallimard, 1961), 191–244, for a full discussion of Stendhal's fascination with pseudonyms.

4. *Oeuvres intimes*, ed. Victor del Litto (Paris: Gallimard, 1982), 1415–16.

5. One of his recent critics, Nicholas Rand, has seen in this choice of a pseudonym a specific and premonitory gloss on the ending of *The Red and the Black*: "Marie-Henri Beyle, a French author, borrows a German name and adds to it a silent *h*. Unspoken in the pseudonym itself, this letter can be given its full name in the French alphabet: *hache*, whose homonym means "axe" in French. If we read *hache* (axe) in the name Stendhal, which heads *The Red and the Black*, this pseudonym . . . can be seen . . . hiding a reference to the guillotine" ("*The Red and the Black*, Author of Stendhal: Pseudonyms and Cryptonyms of Beyle," *Romanic Review* 80, no. 3 [May 1989]: 391–403).

6. Roy, *Stendhal*, 41. My translation.

7. Friedrich Nietzsche, *On the Genealogy of Morals / Ecce Homo*, trans. Walter Kaufmann (New York: Vintage, 1969), 244.

8. Quoted in Harold Bloom, ed., *Modern Critical Interpretations: the Red and the Black* (New York: Chelsea House, 1988), 1.

9. Ann Jefferson, "Stendhal and the Uses of Reading: *Le Rouge et le noir*," in Bloom, 94.

10. René Girard, "*The Red and the Black*: Deceit and Desire," in Bloom, 23.

11. Peter Brooks, "The Novel and the Guillotine; or, Fathers and Sons in *Le Rouge et le noir*," in Bloom, 78.

12. D. A. Miller, "Narrative 'Uncontrol' in Stendhal," in Bloom, 35, 55.

13. Georges Poulet, *Mesure de l'instant* (Paris: Plon, 1968), 250; Quoted in translation in Paul de Man, *Blindness and Insight* (Minneapolis: University of Minnesota Press, 1983), 227.

14. Barbara Johnson, *The Critical Difference* (Baltimore: Johns Hopkins University Press, 1980), 146.

15. Paul de Man, "The Rhetoric of Temporality," in *Blindness and Insight*, 210–11. My emphasis.

16. Baton Rouge, Louisiana, *Morning Advocate*, 19 September 1989, p. 1.

17. Brooks, "The Novel and the Guillotine."

18. See Rand, "*The Red and the Black*, Author of Stendhal."

19. Shoshana Felman, *La Folie dans l'oeuvre romanesque de Stendhal* (Paris: José Corti, 1971), 162. My translation.

20. Jefferson, "Stendhal and the Uses of Reading," 128.

21. This discussion owes much to Jean Laplanche's study *Vie et mort en psychanalyse* (Paris: Flammarion, 1970), trans. Jeffrey Mehlman as *Life and Death in Psychoanalysis* (Baltimore: Johns Hopkins University Press, 1976). Laplanche demonstrates that Freud's distinction between Eros (life instinct) and Thanatos (death instinct) functions as a chiasmus. Peter Brooks develops some literary consequences of this idea in "Freud's Masterplot: Questions of Narrative," *Yale French Studies* 55/56 (1977): 280–300. See also Frank Kermode, *The Sense of an Ending* (New York: Oxford University Press, 1967).

Selected Bibliography

Primary Works in French

Collected Works

Correspondance. Edited by Henri Martineau and Victor del Litto. 3 vols. Paris: Gallimard (Bibliothèque de la Pléiade), 1962–68.

Oeuvres intimes. Edited by Victor del Litto. Paris: Gallimard (Bibliothèque de la Pléiade), 1982.

Romans et nouvelles. Edited by Henri Martineau. 2 vols. Paris: Gallimard (Bibliothèque de la Pléiade), 1952.

Novels

La Chartreuse de Parme. Edited by Antoine Adam. Paris: Classiques Garnier, 1973.

Le Rouge et le Noir. Edited by P.-G. Castex. Paris: Classiques Garnier, 1973.

Primary Works in English (Major Novels)

The Charterhouse of Parma. Translated by C. K. Scott-Moncrief. New York: Modern Library, 1925.

The Red and the Black. Translated by Lloyd C. Parks. New York: Signet Classics/New American Library, 1970.

Secondary Works

Books

Bardèche, Maurice. *Stendhal romancier*. Paris: Editions de la Table Ronde, 1947. An excellent study of Stendhal's mind and craft as a writer, marred by extreme right-wing political orientation.

Bloom, Harold, ed. *Modern Critical Interpretations: Stendhal's "The Red and the Black."* New York: Chelsea House, 1988. An excellent anthology of recent criticism on the novel.

Brombert, Victor. *Stendhal: Fiction and Themes of Freedom*. New York: Random House, 1968. A thematic study of the major novels and the Italian stories.

————, ed. *Stendhal: A Collection of Critical Essays*. Englewood Cliffs, N.J.: Prentice-Hall, 1962. Somewhat dated and old-fashioned, but still a useful collection of critical essays.

————. *Stendhal et la voie oblique*. New Haven, Conn.: Yale University Press, 1954. Focuses on Stendhal's frequent parenthetical intrusions, as narrator, in his fictional works.

Brooks, Peter. *Reading for the Plot: Design and Intention in Narrative*. New York: Knopf, 1984. Includes a useful psychoanalytic/narratological reading of *The Red and the Black*.

Del Litto, Victor. *La Vie intellectuelle de Stendhal*. Paris: Presses Universitaires de France, 1959. The definitive intellectual biography; an exhaustive study of the evolution of Stendhal's writing style and personal philosophy.

Felman, Shoshana. *La Folie dans l'oeuvre romanesque de Stendhal*. Paris: Corti, 1971. A thematic, linguistic, and psychoanalytic study of "madness" in the fiction of Stendhal, concentrating on *Armance* and *La Chartreuse de Parme*.

Fowlie, Wallace. *Stendhal*. New York: Macmillan, 1969. A general introduction to the life and work, including basic summaries of the most important works.

Girard, René. *Deceit, Desire, and the Novel*. Baltimore: Johns Hopkins University Press, 1965. Contains an indispensable chapter on the way in which mimetic desire works in *The Red and the Black*.

Gutwirth, Marcel. *Stendhal*. Boston: Twayne, 1971. A brief introductory work.

Jefferson, Ann. *Reading Realism in Stendhal*. Cambridge: Cambridge

University Press, 1988. An excellent theoretical study of the ideology of realistic representation as practiced by Stendhal.

Martineau, Henri. *Le Coeur de Stendhal.* Paris: Albin Michel, 1952–53. Considered the definitive biography.

————. *L'Oeuvre de Stendhal.* Paris: Albin Michel, 1951. An account of how each work was conceived and evolved.

————. *Petit dictionnaire stendhalien.* A glossary of names mentioned in all of the works.

Mossman, Carol A. *The Narrative Matrix: Stendhal's "Le Rouge et le Noir."* Lexington, Ky.: French Forum, 1984. A psychological (Freudian) and narratological approach.

Roy, Claude. *Stendhal.* Paris: Ecrivains de Toujours/Seuil, 1951. Excellent general introduction to life and work.

Articles

Rand, Nicholas. "*The Red and the Black*, Author of Stendhal: Pseudonyms and Cryptonyms of Beyle." *Romanic Review* 80, no. 3 (May 1989): 391–403. A fascinating discussion of the significance and origin of Beyle's pseudonym.

Starobinski, Jean. "Stendhal pseudonyme." In *L'Oeil vivant,* 191–244. Paris: Gallimard, 1961. A seminal essay on Stendhal's affinity for pseudonyms.

Index

Index

The Author

Jefferson Humphries is professor of French, English, and comparative literature at the Louisiana State University. Educated at Duke and Yale universities, he is the author of *The Puritan and the Cynic: The Literary Moralist in America and France* (1987), *Losing the Text: Readings in Literary Desire* (1986), *Metamorphoses of the Raven: Literary Overdeterminedness in France and the South since Poe* (1985), and *The Otherness Within: Gnostic Readings in Marcel Proust, Flannery O'Connor, and François Villon* (1983). He edited *Southern Literature and Literary Theory* (1990), and his stories and poems have appeared in many literary magazines and anthologies.